THE COMP ⊔ᴜᴵᴅᴇ
TO SELF AWARENESS

THE COMPREHENSIVE GUIDE TO SELF AWARENESS

Guidance from the Source

Beatrice McCaig

© Beatrice McCaig 2009

Published by Beatrice McCaig

ISBN: 978-0-9564599-0-9

A CIP catalogue record for this book is available from the British Library.

Prepared by:

York Publishing Services Ltd
64 Hallfield Road
Layerthorpe
York YO31 7ZQ
Tel: 01904 431213

Website: www.yps-publishing.co.uk

DEDICATION

I dedicate this book to those who work tirelessly, both in this world, and the next, to bring us the knowledge that life is eternal, that you cannot be separated from those you love, that the consciousness lives on, and survives the death of the physical body.

To the hundreds of energies both incarnate and discarnate who are working to give us an understanding of the power we hold within us.

The ability, therefore, to make changes within our lives, for the betterment of all who journey this universe.

But, mostly, to The Source of all existence, the omnipresent energies that are ever constantly guiding and enlightening us, helping us to know who we really are and our purpose in this and the next life.

ACKNOWLEDGEMENTS

A big THANK YOU to my two friends Leona Janice Graham and Warren Boswell for all their encouragement, words of wisdom and dedication in helping make this book possible.

For the beautiful and professional design of the book's cover – I could not have wished for better. You are truly two very special people and it is a great pleasure to know and work with you both.

***

To the two psychical researchers involved in the paranormal experiments, thank you, for giving me the opportunity to work with such professional, dedicated people on the experiments undertaken.

Archibald A. Lawrie,

Professional Psychical Researcher,

President, Edinburgh Society for Psychical Research.

Vice-President, Scottish Society for Psychical Research.

Ann Treherne,

Psychical Researcher, Edinburgh Society for Psychical Research.

***

To my dear husband Frank, my two sons, grandson and granddaughter for your love, patience and incredible support, my grateful thanks.

INTRODUCTION

I have been involved in many aspects of the paranormal for over two decades.

Born in the small mining village of Prestonpans on the east coast of Scotland. I was aware from early childhood of being sensitive to other people's feelings/sufferings – not seeing or hearing, just knowing.

In 1982 my mother died. The day she died was the saddest day of my life. My mother knew she was dying and wanted to talk to me about it but my courage failed me although I DID know how to help her come to terms with her death. I visited her in the funeral parlour to say goodbye but the only feeling I had was her voice in my head telling me "This is not the end. It is the beginning".

This of course, set me on the journey I was destined to take. A search that has taken me twenty five years. Since then I have jointly conducted a funeral service and read several eulogies.

After my mother's death I joined a spiritualist church, sat in development groups seeking knowledge whatever way was available.

It took several more years of study to understand the workings of the psychic worlds. At around this time I became the founder/president of the Dawn of Light Spiritualist Church in my local area for five years. My next appointment was tutor/demonstrator at the Edinburgh College of Parapsychology.

In 1999 I was awakened one morning by a very clear discarnate male voice telling me "You are moving". This surprised me as I do not normally hear the psychic world. I only sense it. The move was to England. This was a difficult decision as it involved uprooting my dear husband. However with his support we sold up and made the move.

We lived there for two years, during which time I served several churches, took meditation groups and started a home circle for self awareness and worked for a few charity events. During that time I attained my Diploma in Hypnotherapy and my Reiki Masters Degree.

To my amazement, I kept hearing clairaudiently that my next move would be connected to Spain. I love Spain and enjoyed the work immensely. I also made many good friends during that time all of whom still play an important part in my life today

I held healing and psychic development groups, one to one private readings, reiki attunement courses and once a month I gave a demonstration of clairvoyance in aid of the Cudeca Charity and I was granted an interview with Spanish Radio. I still travel back regularly to work; my work has also taken me to California and San Diego several times.

Since returning to Scotland I am serving the Edinburgh Association of Spiritualists as a committee member. Before moving away I was Vice-President of the Association and look upon it as my home Church.

I have always known it is possible to go into the future to obtain information and I am now very much involved in Paranormal Research which is thoroughly fascinating and very challenging.

My journey has been and is one of many experiences and emotions – joy, frustration, patience, humour, love, and sadness. I have experienced them all but I would not have changed them for the world as they have made me the person I am today – a happy medium with the ability to share my experiences with others so that they can find their way and know that they too can achieve their goals whatever they may be.

SECTION 1

Power of observation

How mediums and psychics work

Twenty fun questions on personal development

Enhance your personal development

Self-attunement

Introduction to healing

Spiritual and reiki healing – energy work

Energy

Telepathy

Hypnosis

Psychic/mediumistic development quiz

POWER OF OBSERVATION

1. Are you shy?

2. Have you a good sense of right and wrong?

3. Do you have a feeling that you are more than just a physical body?

4. Have you ever been about to telephone a friend only to discover at the same time they are phoning you?

5. When you dream, have you ever experienced that the dream has become a reality?

6. As a child, did you have imaginary friends?

7. Are you in tune with other people's thoughts and emotions?

8. When you are alone, have you ever been aware of the smell of tobacco or perfume, or heard loud rappings?

9. Can you sense when someone is ill?

10. Do you either like or dislike a person instantly?

11. Are you aware of colour around people?

12. Have you ever seen objects move in your presence without any physical assistance?

13. Can you sense impending danger, before it happens?

14. Does electrical equipment go wrong around you?

15. Are you aware of spirit consciousness?

16. Do you enjoy silence?

17. Have you felt at any time that you are aware of what someone will say next, or you can finish their sentence?

18. Upon entering a room are you aware of different vibrations, changes in atmosphere?

19. Do extreme noises upset you?

20. Do you astral travel? Have you ever thought you can travel outside your physical body?

Please answer all the questions – you will find that some relate to yourself and are helpful in your further development.

If you require assistance with any of these questions or any other questions you may have, then please consult my website www.beatricemccaig.com for further help.

HOW MEDIUMS AND PSYCHICS WORK

Think of yourself as the channel for information and liken that to a computer, and when you know which buttons to press you will be taken to the right link to receive the information. In today's terms, you can relate to Google, as the main source of information, and once acquainted with guidance you can begin to develop knowledge, taking a step at a time, at your own pace, searching the many links that lead to spiritual development. Google can symbolise consciousness and help in your search.

I do believe in the saying. "When the pupil is ready the master will appear".

We must firstly get to know who we are, before we can move on to knowing the possibilities of communicating with other source energies on a psychic, mediumistic, channelling level. We must learn about the universal consciousness and its entire links to be able to bring forward communication to this earthly vibration.

Therefore whilst in this physical body, you are on a spiritual venture to find yourself and thereby, in time, have no need to ask the question which haunts most of us. – Who Am I?

A good starting point would be to find yourself a good, reputable spiritual teacher, who is willing to assist you in your search for truths, someone whom you trust and feel comfortable with, and of course, not too expensive, for your search must be one of joy, but I do warn you that you will come across a few stumbling blocks, but please, keep in mind, that they are there for a reason and it is your quest to find out what that reason is.

I wish you luck with your search and I do know that you will eventually find what you are searching or surfing for in the end.

Let me leave you with these thoughts:-

"Be careful what you ask for, as you might just get it".

"Positive thoughts create positive things".

Psychic:

Firstly let me ask you a question – "Are you psychic"? The answer is, of course, yes. Everybody is psychic. It is something you are born with, it is part of who you really are and cannot be separated from. It is the part of you which is connected to the universal source energy which is infinite, it is who you are now, have been and always will be. There is a power within that can connect to that source energy whilst here on this earthly vibration, with the ability to connect to other source energy beings through the psyche. When you sit for meditation and try to attune yourself to that source then you will become at one with the power, which can be used to enhance your life and also the lives of others whilst on this earthly vibration.

Medium:

I have worked for many years as a medium. My interpretation of a medium is a person who can receive and channel communications from source energy on many levels. The first level is having the ability to listen to our own energy, remembering energy equals thoughts, in order to enhance our own lives while on this earthly vibration we also need to be able to link into source energy of other people, known as incarnate energy, so that we may pass on information to and from each other – known as psychic.

Then we have discarnate energy. When there is no longer a physical body, only a consciousness we can as mediums/channels attune our psyche to receive communication from the universal discarnate source energies to pass on to incarnate beings on this earthly vibration, therefore confirming that consciousness lives on after what we call physical death.

All mediums are psychic but not all psychics are mediums. I partly agree with the maxim as we all have the ability to raise our vibrational level to attune ourselves with discarnate energies on many levels, hence we become our own medium or channel.

Be happy in the knowledge that consciousness is ever in existence, as it is the energy force within each and every living thing and therefore, has been, is, will be, ever present. Use that force to enhance your life and the lives of others you have the good fortune to touch upon.

TWENTY FUN QUESTIONS ON PERSONAL DEVELOPMENT

Answer all questions with Yes or No – My results appear at the back of the book. – Have Fun.

Are you a sensitive?	Y/N
Do you know who you really are?	Y/N
Do you know what intuition is?	Y/N
Do you meditate?	Y/N
Do you use visualisation exercises at any time?	Y/N
Are you aware of universal energies?	Y/N
Do you believe in a discarnate supreme being?	Y/N
Can you contact your inner- self?	Y/N
Are you telepathic?	Y/N
Do you have an aura?	Y/N
Are you a good judge of character?	Y/N
Do you believe the consciousness lives on after the death of the physical body?	Y/N
Is it possible to foresee the future?	Y/N
Do you know what precognition is?	Y/N
Do you think you have lived a previous life?	Y/N
Have you ever been under hypnosis?	Y/N

Do you believe it is possible to cure yourself of certain illnesses? Y/N

Do you believe the mind is more powerful than the physical body? Y/N

Do you believe there is a parallel universe? Y/N

Are you really sure you want to further develop your psychic awareness? Y/N

ENHANCE YOUR PERSONAL DEVELOPMENT

Let me share this thought with you:

Have you ever had one of those days when you wished your world would just end, so you could find some peace?

When everything you do, say, try, hope for, seems to be wrong, can't get anything right, you are in utter desperation, through no fault of your own, so you think.

I can just hear you say, woe is me.

So what are you going to do about it?

The answer of course, is find out who you really are, and why so many things appear to be going wrong in your life. As you must always keep in mind the saying – "Like Attracts Like" as that is the Universal Law of Attraction.

Your search must therefore come from within to find your psyche, the ability to attune yourself to source energies, to find out what makes you the person you appear to be.

It is only when you become attuned to your own source, sometimes referred to as incarnate, spirit, soul, psyche, mediumistic or whatever you feel most comfortable with, you will find peace of mind. The simplest, easiest way is by relaxation, meditation, positive thinking, affirmations, and learning how to love yourself and share that with others.

When you become attuned to your own source energy and are more confident about whom you are, then things do not seem to be so severe and whatever occurrences come your way good or bad, you can begin to see them in a more positive way, thereby making you more able to cope with life in general. Once you have taken that huge step, which is rightly yours, in finding yourself, then there is no going back, things just begin to get better and better and nothing will seem the same again.

When all things come together, mind, body and spirit, we become the whole package, and nothing can separate us from who we really are, a wonderful human being, placed upon this earthly plane, source energy encased within a physical body, until such time as we wish to join once again with discarnate energies on life's journey, but of course, that is only when we have fulfilled our earthly desires.

Let me just give you this thought. – What you recognise in others, might well be an image of yourself, for that is the only way you can recognise it, so try and always seek for the best in those whom you meet throughout your earthly life, try at least once a day to make someone happy, if you can't find something nice to say, then don't say anything at all.

SELF-ATTUNEMENT

When I began teaching, I tried different methods of meditation until I discovered four simple steps, relaxation, visualization, dedication and meditation, which I still use in my workshops today.

Relaxation:

Allow yourself time to relax your physical body. Sit comfortably, close your eyes and become aware of the rhythm of your breathing. Listening to music is beneficial in letting go the thoughts of the day and gives you the pleasure of your own time.

Relaxation can be done anywhere at any time and if practised, even for a few minutes each day, your life will be enhanced.

Visualisation:

Find a quiet spot, tune into your breathing and visualize within your mind's eye, a flower, a crystal, or any symbol you feel comfortable with, to hold your focus and still your mind. Acknowledge any thoughts that arise, let them go and return to your focus. Visualization trains the mind for the many different levels of communication available. As the mind develops further, you become aware that your thoughts are perhaps discarnate thought forms you can receive through the stillness of your mind.

Dedication:

Probably the most important of the steps to become attuned to in order to reach the many vibrational levels for communication to take place be that with your consciousness or that of source energy. It is essential that time is set aside each day to sit in quietness.

Meditation

Meditation is the art of setting oneself free from material thoughts and cares of the day to achieve an altered state of consciousness for the benefit of the sitter. Meditation should become a way of life. It should be practised every day until it is a very important part of who you are for it is only in silence the greatness of one can be achieved. Many of you will have experienced memories of altered states of consciousness through meditation, the dream state, or perhaps hypnosis.

When you sit in meditation you create the vibrations possible for change to take place and when you have attuned yourself to the light within you know you are a part of the greater universe.

There have been many great Seers on the earth plane in the past, but never before has there been such a great opportunity for enlightenment as we approach many changes on our earthly plane – the way is clear for all who wish to embark upon this road.

We live in a time when we will see a coming together of all universes for the greater good of all. The only thing that is asked of you is to take the light and share it with others, for you have all chosen to be ambassadors of the light, not by mistake, but by choice.

Enjoy the journey, it is yours for the taking, it is in abundance and not reserved for the chosen few, but for all who wish to become attuned to what is rightfully theirs. I believe as vibrational source energy our hopes and desires are unlimited and available to all who search for answers. The universe receives and returns your thoughts, and will try to act upon your desires. So be careful what you ask for as you may just get it.

INTRODUCTION TO HEALING

I have worked as a healer for many years. It was the first thing that brought me to study spiritualism, which is another field that holds great interest for me. I was unwell and not making any progress with conventional medicine. However I found myself in a spiritualist church, for spiritual healing, recommended to me by a good friend. I must admit I was rather sceptical, but thought, what have I to lose I will go along anyway, out of curiosity.

Thank goodness I did, whilst I did not see right away any physical changes within me, I soon realised I felt much better within my mind and more relaxed about my illnesses, which led me to further explore spiritual healing, which in turn led me to reiki healing.

After much studying, I have come to the conclusion that when we are attuned to the universe then healing will take place on many levels. We each of us hold the power within, to help heal us on many levels of consciousness, physical, mental, emotional, spiritual and to use the power of thought to bring about a balance within our physical body thereby enhancing our daily lives and giving us the inner strength to cope with whatever comes our way, whether that be body, mind, or consciousness.

All of these things and more can be used to become attuned to source energy and the universe. Just thought I would let you know, I am perfectly healthy to date, so please don't feel too sorry for me, but I do appreciate any nice thoughts sent my way, for my philosophy is that "Positive thoughts create positive things" and it works.

SPIRITUAL AND REIKI HEALING − ENERGY WORK

Develop As A Healer:

If you are interested in becoming a healer, no matter what source you choose i.e. spiritual, reiki, contact, reflexology, hypnotherapy, psychology, there are so many choices.

Attunement:

To enhance your connection to the universal energy, you must make sure that you research the source you wish to use thoroughly, check your tutor comes highly recommended and knows their subject. Be very careful of people who ask for extortionate fees for your tutoring, as universal energy is FREE and there for the use of anyone who wishes to take the time to find it for themselves.

Working With Healing Energies:

You must firstly become attuned to your own energy source before you begin to work with others as you are dealing with, in some cases, very vulnerable people who see you as there last hope for the future.

You must be able to work with people's emotions without it having too much effect upon yourself in order to be able to help them and also remain rooted in the thought that you are only ever a channel for any healing to take place.

Personal Responsibility:

If you decide this is the pathway you wish to take, you must be aware of the responsibility you hold within you as a healer and it's not to be entered into lightly, if done for the wrong reasons you will do more damage than good.

My Personal Views On Healing

Having studied several different methods of healing, I soon realised that the only way to help anyone is just to be an open channel for source energy, to enable that energy to connect to the recipient. The way that this is done, for me, is through my conscious thoughts being sent to the recipient.

I do not think it is right for a healer to take away the recipient's freedom of choice by asking the source for what you want for them, you can only ask for what is needed for them and hope that it has a positive effect.

Diagnosis:

It would be very wrong as a healer to try to diagnose what the recipient's problems are, whether they are mental, physical or emotional. Because as in all probability you will pick up that information psychically and it may well be that you have picked up what the person thinks is wrong with them, when in fact it might be something completely different.

Choose Carefully:

I think before your final choice it would be a good idea to test the water, by trying several complimentary therapies and not focus too much on one until you find what suits you best.

Good luck in your search, remain positive and go with your own gut feeling, remembering "positive thoughts create positive things".

ENERGY

The source of all being is ENERGY which is of no particular substance as it is not of this physical world, but of the non-physical world. It is a source of vibrations on many levels operating at speeds, in tune with whatever your thoughts are at any given time and the ability you have to attune yourself to your own source energy, for only you hold the key to this knowledge.

To understand energy you must first understand that we are all energy beings. Whilst in the earthly body, that body is made up of earthly matter – brain, heart, kidneys, liver and so on, as that is what is needed for the physical body to survive the earthly vibrations, but they are of no significance when dealing with the energy source that is really you. When you begin to understand that energy operates on many, many levels and in many, many different ways, things will be clearer to you.

Let us begin by saying you have come to this earthly plane and taken up a physical form for your journey, for however long, which again is earthly time, you wish to be here, to experience what you have laid out for yourself.

At this point in earth time it is my understanding that I am here to fulfil the pathway that I have set out for myself, whether that be in earthly terms, good or bad, as I believe from my energy source that good and bad are only a balancing of vibrations. Where there is one you will find the other.

I hear people speak of the new energy which has come to this earth plane, but I believe that there is nothing new about energy as it is, was and will be, and who we really are.

What is happening on our earth is that our awareness of energy has been brought more to the fore and more and more people are beginning to research the power that lies within these energies.

TELEPATHY

All communications from The Source on all levels are done in a telepathic manner, as the mind is the only tool available to us at this moment to impart communications to your world.

It is the one thing that survives the death of the physical body and it can be used on many, many, different levels, depending upon the attunement of the channel.

There is no need for earthly beings to keep striving endlessly in a search for something to prove that you are more than physical beings, you only have to look to yourself for the answer, as no one else understands you better than you.

You came forward to this earthly vibration with all the necessary equipment you need whilst here for your experiences of this world. And when you realize that you yourself are the channel to the inner and outer worlds then your life span here on this earth will be a much happier and fulfilled one.

You constantly search for answers in a physical way asking for physical proof to be shown, proof that you can see, touch, hear, smell, and speak. You can achieve all these things through your own sensitivity by allowing yourself to come into line with the inner and outer worlds.

You have been conditioned on this earthly plane to think as those who have gone before and your life is a constant search for truths when in actual fact everything is so, so simple, but you try to put labels and attachments to everything in order to understand in a physical way, when in fact you are a physical being with a non-physical attachment to source, YOU.

If you are seeking clever answers to the many questions, we say to you, what a waste of your earthly time, be happy with your life and enjoy your experiences for you have chosen them, before you came to this earth.

We must learn to appreciate this earth plane for what it is, a beautiful existence willing to share its many beauties.

We in the outer worlds watch you struggle in trying to come to terms with your world and we do what we can to help in whatever way is possible, but if you would only really listen to your inner telepathic thoughts from source then there would be no struggle, only a happy contented human being.

HYPNOSIS

Hypnosis is an extremely powerful therapy and can be dangerous in the wrong hands. If you decide to explore this avenue of the mind for your own development, please make sure you consult a qualified, recommended clinical hypnotherapist.

I have studied and worked with clinical hypnosis in many development groups, and in my search for – who am I, using self-hypnosis to attune my mind to the many states of meditation with some interesting results. It is always good to search for answers in whatever ways seem right and comfortable for you. There are a multitude of choices available to the serious researcher, these are only my experiences I share with you and hopefully you will find the path which works for you. Happy hunting, have fun.

PSYCHIC/MEDIUMISTIC
DEVELOPMENT QUIZ

STATE WHETHER TRUE OR FALSE – ANSWERS AT
THE BACK OF THE BOOK

Should psychic/mediumistic development be open to
anyone?

Do you have to be psychic to become a medium?

Would you attempt to first make your mind clear when
sitting for development?

Can a medium follow any religion they choose?

Should you encourage a developing medium to work with
their eyes closed?

Can you sit in different development circles as often as you
please?

Would you ever apologise for your mediumship?

Would you always give evidence of communicator?

Whilst sitting in development circles how clear are you of
what type of mediumship you wish to have?

Do you have to have spiritual knowledge to develop physical
phenomena?

When in trance is the mind of the medium highly active?

Do you think you should ever question what your tutor
tells you?

SECTION 2

Is the law of attraction as important as we think it is?

What is most stuck In my vibration which stops me from moving faster into what I want?

QUESTIONS AND ANSWERS FOR THE SOURCE

The Future

How is it possible, to go into the future six months in advance and be able to tell who will be in a certain room, and sitting in a certain place, on a certain date and see specific details of what that person is wearing?

Also how is it possible, to see their future six months in advance if they themselves are not even aware that they would be at that place, on that date, at that time themselves, at that point?

Also to be able to give them a communication from their deceased loved ones about what is going on in the recipient's life at that time and proof of survival that the consciousness lives on after the death of the physical body?

Answers Received

There is nothing new happening on your earthly vibration, as it has all happened already, as you yourself have set it forth before you came to this earthly plane to experience your desires, and have now come forward to experience them in this physical body.

You have set the pattern of your desires from a space and time, not of your physical world, but a source that has no physical substance.

In terms of your earthy vibrations, everything, is of a physical matter.

Whilst in the outer worlds everything is possible by thought, as that is what you are made up from, vibrational energy, thoughts.

You are not new to anything, but have been in existence since what you call time, the beginning, and have had many experiences of the inner and outer worlds.

When you once more become in tune to source energy, then you have the ability to move in any direction you chose, as there are no restrictions placed upon you by The Source. You impose the restriction of time to experience your desires before coming to this earthly vibration and when you no longer have the desire or use for time then you leave this earthly vibration and return once again to source.

Time is the greatest restriction you place upon yourself, as it is of this earthly plane, but when you are connected to The Source then you are an unlimited being, source encased within a physical body and you can perceive the outer and inner worlds without the intrusion of time as you know it.

Finance

As your physical world moves forward into the future, there will be many changes on this earthly vibration, a lot of very difficult financial times ahead which are necessary for the growth of your world as it is a way forward in joining all people of this earthly vibration to the understanding that when you pool your resources from all aspects then your world will be able to survive this economic crisis.

We in the outer worlds can only use the things that are available to us from our earthly perspective one of which is, of course, money. Although all things seem to be negative from our physical point of view at this time, of course that is not so, it is a great time to bring everyone together in harmony and understanding.

We are trying to make you aware of the possibilities that can be achieved on your earthly plane when you become enlightened. You are not just a physical body searching for financial assets and a comfortable lifestyle, all life is a gift to be cherished and brought into alignment with the very source of your being. More and more people are becoming attuned to the thoughts that life is everlasting and we will all achieve this, but you must firstly bring yourself into attunement.

The people of your earthly world have for many, many years of your time been trying to analyse the inner and outer worlds and have given that analysis many names, mostly done under the auspices of religion. Of course, it is not possible to name things you do not yet fully understand. You are physical beings encased within a physical body with a non-physical attachment to the very source of your being.

You from a physical point of view restrict yourselves in many ways, because you focus all your thoughts on physical things. It is only when you start to search within the inner worlds your own psyche, that you can begin to understand that there is also a restriction going on, as you feel attached to the worlds closest to your understanding. Until you are ready to move on to the outer worlds beyond consciousness and become part of the source you really are, then things begin to change in your world and material assets become less important.

It is very difficult for you earthly beings to understand at times the way of the outer worlds, but we are patient and always willing to help, but, of course, we remain restricted in what we can do for earth, as it is about freedom of choice and the willingness to change your way of thinking and once again return to The Source you really are.

When adequate numbers work on the same vibration then it is possible to make these changes for the improvement of your world.

Of course, we will try to help you in any way possible. We are always willing to assist in whatever way we can as we too learn from your world thus making communications easier for you in bringing all the many worlds together under one source. It can be done if you are all willing to work together.

Do You Understand your Own Power?

Each of you holds within you the power to be anything you desire to be. When you hold yourself in tune with the vibrational being that you really are, all things become possible.

You must firstly acknowledge that you are human beings encased within a physical body with a non-physical attachment to The Source. You came here on a physical life journey to recapture your identity to enable you to enhance your source energy.

You came asking many questions, but what you do not realise is that you, set the course of these questions, before you came to this earthly vibration, you are only here to experience what you have already laid down.

The one thing that you all desire is the need to be loved, as love is the greatest physical emotion of all. The emotion that you can feel, see and sense all around you, if you look in the right direction.

Learn to love yourself and you will indeed love the whole universe on many levels.

You hold within you the power to make others happy or sad – that is your choice, but when you focus on the positive and always look for the best then that is what you will receive.

Do not be afraid to be different. Your world needs you to bring about changes and it is only when you are heard and your presence felt that others can became attuned to you and their own source.

Be confident, be strong, go in search of you and find the peace from within, enjoy your experience here on your earthly plane, and spread your knowledge around whenever you have the opportunity for that is the purpose of your journey.

Help those who may be troubled and come your way, be the leader of others in making changes for the benefit of all.

All we ask is that you be happy, to be unhappy creates negativity.

What is Time?

Time is your reality; it has nothing to do with the universe as you know it. You have created this vibration within this time space world you live in. It is not of our universe but is necessary for your understanding of your world.

When you talk of time you talk of a condition within your earthly plane and are of no significance in our world. We try and perceive your questions as to what you think time is in a logical and understandable way so that it is made simpler for you as earthly beings to understand what we mean.

You must try to forget about time, whilst you connect to the inner/outer worlds which you are striving to reach, as it holds no purpose.

I must tell you, that the understanding of time as we know it, will not be achieved on your earthly vibration for many, many years as you are not ready to receive this knowledge, there are very few at this moment who understand what we mean; only those who know of consciousness travel.

All consciousness, incarnate/discarnate can move forward and back within the universe, as time holds no restrictions. Know what you are at this moment, who you will always be, and more.

You are indeed universal travellers and always have been, you know many other dimensions and are not restricted to this earthly plane, you have been sent here for a purpose and that purpose is to assist the universe in their development of the greater plan for mankind, all things will be made clearer to you in due course.

After you ask many questions and receive many answers, you are ready to accept that you have the ability to do our work and be recognised as a universal traveller.

There will be many things that you will be asked to do and we will be there to guide and assist you, do not be afraid of what is coming forward for your world.

There is no need to push forward as we have taken a lot of care to put you where you are at this moment and that is the correct place, trust in us and we will help you to understand the non-understandable.

What we have to say is very, very important for the advancement of your earthly world. You are a light in the dark. Over time there have been many changes within your vibrational planet with still more to come. You will emerge stronger and know the channel you are.

Know that you can be on any vibrational level that you choose and not be restricted by time or the physical body.

How do I know there is a Greater Spirit?

When you do not have to ask that question, is when all things will be clear to you.

The answer lies within yourself, when you know and understand the spiritual being that you really are. It will not come about through searching all physical avenues, but through patience and finding your inner source.

Search within your inner and outer worlds for your answers, because only you can answer what you desire. Every path you walk on this earthly vibration takes you closer to The Source, and makes your search easier by looking to yourself.

Your source does not have to prove anything to you, as you have the answers within, trust yourself, and become attuned to you, when that happens then the outer worlds will be closer than you ever thought possible.

The Source cannot interfere with your desires, your search must be within, but you must make that search a joyful one, as your source wishes that for you.

Enjoy your earthly journey and share your experiences with others.

Do You See a More Positive Change Coming About on on this Early Vibrations?

When sufficient numbers are in harmony with each other a more positive vibration will be created and your earthly plane will indeed benefit from the positive thoughts. Energies can be changed allowing the beautiful world to emerge.

There is a darkness surrounding the planet at this time and the harmony will allow change to take place in order to create the beautiful world it was always meant to be.

We will not take away anyone's free-will, or freedom of choice, because that is your right. You must look at your world and your attitude as to how you perceive your world to be, before you can make any changes.

Each of you put forward your desires before you came to this earthly vibration for whatever experience you wished to have.

The Source will not, and can not take away your free-will, only you have the choice of what you desire.

Will I Continue To Learn Whilst In Another State Of Consciousness?

Always, YES, but there are many altered states of consciousness and depending upon your understanding of what you are asking for, will depend on the answer you receive.

Firstly, let me try to help you understand that all life is a circle of learning and we each receive what is needed for us at any given time.

We all vibrate at different levels and therefore our understanding is dependent upon what our vibrational level is.

There is no negative thoughts only negative understanding and when you are ready to receive the knowledge then it will be given to you.

Progression is ever in existence, and there for all who seek it.

May I say, that on all levels of consciousness you do not have to learn anything, because you know all things already, the only thing you have to do is align yourself to the source energy that you really are, and all answers are within your vibration, you have only just forgotten them whilst in this physical body, they are not lost only in abeyance until you are ready to accept them into your vibration once again.

Why Is There So Much Suffering As Part Of Life?

This is a very difficult question to answer, as there is no suffering to the real you The Source, only experiences of the physical body. You may find these answers rather difficult to understand, but you, in your Source form asked to experience whatever you desired before you came to this physical body and earthly plane.

You are never asked to endure any more than the physical body can withstand, as you have the freedom to leave that body behind whenever you choose, because that is your right.

You ask for experiences good or bad from a physical perspective, but these experiences can only enhance the real you and bring about a better understanding of who you really are.

Sometimes, what you believe to be negative, can work out to be the opposite and bring about many great changes on your earth plane. Often, when, what appear to be major disasters in your world happen, that is when you all come together in harmony and love, so was the disaster meant, or not, I ask you?

The only thing that can bring about change on your earthly planet is harmony and love for one another, without thought for yourself.

Can you do that?

Who Are You?

I am all you desire me to be, I am you, and you are me.

How would I, and can I achieve and maintain conscious communication with the collective consciousness – The Source.

You have conscious communication right here in the moment, because you are using your consciousness to communicate in the now through your mind with The Source. As you put your questions to your source, the communication is being answered, within your consciousness.

You will always have communication with The Source, as it is the life force of which you really are a source you communicate with every day of your existence, wherever you are at any given time or realities, depending upon which vibration you are in. You are the collective consciousness, no need to learn that everyday.

The Source is indeed you, no one person or thing knows more than you do, all knowledge awaits those who have the desires to seek.

Law of Attraction

Many questions have been asked on the law of attraction and the purpose of such a law.

Law of attraction is of your earthly vibration, and nothing to do with The Source, it is a law that you have set in motion whilst in your physical form.

That law will not change your non-physical desires, which you set before you came to this earth plane, as law of attraction, universal law, cosmic law or any other law you wish to talk of has no relevance to The Source.

These laws you have put into place on your earthly vibration to try to understand what you do not yet know. When you have the knowledge that you are The Source then there is no need for any laws.

The Source does not place any restrictions upon you whilst on this earthly vibration, only you do that, but no matter how you try to perceive things from a physical point of view, The Source will not interfere with your intentions.

Law of attraction can bring to you what you desire on this earthly plane, in connection to physical intention, but it cannot interfere with your desires from your non-physical perspective before you came here.

But I would remind you that with the knowledge that you are non-physical source energy encased within a physical body, your desires would not be for what you desire, but for what you can give.

Is the Law of Attraction as important as we may think it is?

To some yes, to others no, for it is only when the recipient is asking the question on law of attraction that they are seeking to know the answers. Not everyone is ready to receive the knowledge of that law whilst still here in their earthly vibration.

How does that law tie in with the thought that we have already decided much of our life experiences before birth?

Only your own understanding of these laws will help you, it will not be seen to help those who have not yet reached that vibrational level. You set out your own patterns of desire, whatever they may be, only you have the power to change your own desires, whether that be in an earthly vibration or whatever level of consciousness you are in.

What is most stuck in my vibration, which stops me from moving faster into what I want?

That is simple, you and your own thoughts!!! Have the patience to allow your vibration to experience its desires.

Your life is not meant to be complicated; you create complications and then wonder how they happened.

Listen to your own guidance system, stay in tune with The Source you really are, do not over complicate things, all things are simple.

Just be the happy energy you were always meant to be.

SECTION 3

Psychic/Mediumistic Development Groups

Psychic Exercises for Self-Development

Exercise 1 – Meditation

Exercise 2 – Colour

Exercise 3 – Flower

Exercise 4 – Deeper stages of meditation

Psychic Groups

Cards

Psychometry

Colour

Assometry

Ouija boards

Table tilting

Psychic experiences

PSYCHIC/MEDIUMISTIC DEVELOPMENT GROUPS

When you feel you are ready to move forward with self-development and begin to encompass psychic development through group work into your vibration you must start to do some ground work and search for the right group you wish to join.

In the beginning it is always a good idea to search around several places that offer group work, for example, spiritualist churches, psychic colleges, self-awareness centres, private tuition till you find somewhere that feels right for you, and you are in harmony with the tutor, as hopefully you will remain there for some considerable time, until you feel it is time to move forward on to the next stage of your development.

I cannot emphasise too much how important it is that you find the right tutor and here are a few pointers, which are important for your development and what you should be looking for.

The tutor has to have his/her feet firmly on the ground with no airy, fairy ideas, that everything is done with harmony, peace and humour, as your journey through development is meant to be a happy one.

You should be able to question any tutor about the group's rules prior to joining. You must ask in the beginning the charge for joining the group and If the class seems too expensive to you, then it usually is, so just go with your gut feeling, bearing in mind, of course, your tutor has to live in the big wide world, and it is their time and experience you are paying for.

It is a good idea that you check with the tutor what experience they have of running development groups and if they are themselves mediumistic, how long they have been working with groups and what you may expect to be taught within the group.

Of course, you do understand that not all groups will accept you right away and may allow you to join for a few weeks trial period, which is only right as the harmony within the group is very important and needs to remain so for the group to progress.

Good luck with your search now let me give you a few ideas as to what you might expect to experience in a psychic development group.

Now that you are well in tune with your own vibration and found the group that you feel is best suited to what you hope to achieve, you are going to begin to connect with other people's vibration on a psychic level through a few mind focus exercises which you might receive whilst in a development group, of course that will very much depend upon the tutor you have chosen.

All tutors have their own way of teaching and nothing is set in stone, there are no set rules on development as each of you will find your own way in attuning yourself, and what is most comfortable to you. Psychic development is ever changing and moving forward as you will discover on your journey for enlightenment.

You must firstly be aware of what vibration you are trying to tune into whilst working with others. When dealing with the psychic vibrations you are tuning into that person's aura on many levels, physical, mental and emotional all things coming together in the psychic reading.

The aura is the vibrational field which is in and around the physical body; it can be seen in a physical way by some mediums as colour around the body, or perhaps just sensed by others. The auric field can also be photographed by a special camera, whereby giving you the opportunity to see the energy field that surrounds each of us, for it is indeed the life-force of the physical body. At this stage I will refer to it as the inner worlds others may call it spirit incarnate.

When you want to attune yourself to read someone on a psychic level you are actually trying to tune into their thought patterns on a mental level which in some cases may be a telepathic level, only through practice will you begin to understand the many levels of communication both with the inner and outer worlds, incarnate or discarnate thoughts.

The ideal number for a group is approximately sixteen students. This is a suitable number for the tutor to work with on a regular basis. As you develop your psychic ability through working with each other, you will pick up information from the group allowing you to practise your mind communication skills.

Ideally, joining an open awareness development group which accepts new members gives you the opportunity to work with different energies.

PSYCHIC EXERCISES FOR
SELF-DEVELOPMENT

In order to prepare for self-development you must become accustomed to meditation on a daily basis, to help you attune to your inner being.

There are many ways of attuning yourself to this vibration and I am sure in time you will find what is best suited to you; meantime, here are a few simple exercises to get you started.

Exercise 1 – Meditation:

Begin by choosing a quiet space where you will not be disturbed for the period you wish to meditate.

Sit in a chair which supports your spine. You may choose to play some relaxing background music. Close your eyes so that you focus inwards.

When you feel comfortable tune into the rhythm of your breathing. Take a deep breath in through the nose, at the same time expand the tummy muscles, hold for a few seconds while visualizing the word peace. As you breathe out through the mouth visualize the word love.

Observe your breathing pattern, do not resist any change that may occur and if your attention drifts bring it back to your breathing.

When you become accustomed and feel comfortable with the above exercise the next step is;

Visualise within your mind's eye a beautiful white pulsating light just above your head. Be aware there is an opening at the crown of your head through which you can visualise the white light passing through.

The light is travelling downwards, through the face, to the neck and shoulder areas, just very slowly, relaxing and soothing as it makes its way down through the physical body. You are aware of any tension in your neck and shoulders beginning to relax, allowing you to release all the tensions of the day.

The light is now travelling down the upper arms, over the elbows, to the lower arms, through to the hands and fingers; you are beginning now to feel more and more relaxed, paying attention to the rhythm of your breathing.

Now visualise that beautiful white light within the chest and heart area, relaxing and soothing the muscles within, bringing you to a more relaxed, happy, contented state of being.

You are aware now of the pulsating white light within the two large muscles on either side of your spine, relaxing and soothing the physical body.

Within your mind's eye see that you are a beautiful white light, as you begin to relax deeper and deeper, aware that you are now beginning to sink back into your chair, almost becoming a part of it.

You become aware now of the white light travelling down into the abdomen and solar plexus area, releasing all tensions, soothing and relaxing as your body now begins to feel just a little heavy.

The white light is travelling down into the large thigh muscles, relaxing and soothing, releasing all tension, travelling downwards over the knees into the calf muscles relaxing and soothing, then onwards over the ankles and into the feet, where you can visualise within your mind the white light now passing through the toes into mother earth thereby making you totally grounded as a being of light.

Sit in the light for however long you feel comfortable with and when you are ready, start to bring your mind back, slowly becoming aware that once again you are bringing your focus back to your physical body, a much more relaxed, happy contented human being.

In the beginning, practise these exercises on a daily basis to visualise yourself as a white light being, ready for whatever circumstances may come your way, now that you can attune yourself to the power that lies within you whenever you choose.

You will begin to notice with the passing of time how much more relaxed you have become through meditation and how much easier it is to cope with life in general now that you have changed within yourself in understanding the real you.

Once you have attuned yourself to that vibration in whatever period of time that may take, please do not try and rush things, all things come in time, you just need patience and when you feel you are ready, then you can move on to the next exercise.

Exercise 2 – Colour:

Now, you are probably aware, after completing and practising Exercise 1 you are more than just a physical body, that you are indeed a wonderful being of white light, you are going to move forward into Exercise 2 and use some visualisation methods to become attuned to your own mind through this practise.

These visualisations can be whatever you choose that will hold your focus, and in time you will find what works best for you, but in the meantime here are a few simple exercises to practise.

As you find yourself once again in your own very quiet space, which you have prepared through the previous exercises in Section 1 you are going on a little journey of the mind.

Within your mind's eye you can visualise a beautiful crystal, you can see very clearly the beautiful colours, the red, orange, yellow, green, blue, purple and white.

If you are having any difficulty with visualising the colour, then just think of the colour in word form which will help your focus. Once you have practised this a few times, it will become much simpler.

I want you to take each colour individually and focus your mind upon it, becoming aware of what you are feeling with each colour as you work your way through them, perhaps being aware of the vibration attached to that colour what it means to you and how it makes you feel inside.

It is important to become aware of colours because they each hold their own vibration and are very much used in the development of psychic and mediumistic awareness, helping you to become attuned to your spiritual side.

When you become attuned to these colours you will realise that you are working with the seven chakras – energy wheels encased within the physical body, they are placed within the body from the crown of the head to the bottom of the spine, going from 1 – 7 or if you prefer 7 – 1.

1. Base Chakra Red.
2. Sacral Orange.
3. Solar Plexus Yellow.
4. Heart Green/Pink.
5. Throat Blue.
6. Forehead Purple/Indigo.
7. Crown White.

Work with each colour individually until you are comfortable with that colour, how it makes you feel, and become aware of the positive attributes the colour brings within your mind.

Visualise that you can expand any colour around your physical body, thereby encasing you in whatever colour or colours you wish to focus upon.

In time these colours will all play a part in your personal development and can be used in the development of psychic and mediumistic attunement.

Exercise 3 – Flower:

Become aware within your mind's eye that you are focused upon a beautiful flower, sense its perfume see its colour and texture and perhaps its shape and form.

Try to hold your focus and acknowledge any spontaneous thoughts you may have and let them go, effortlessly bringing back your focus to the flower or whatever object you have chosen as your focus. It is important to keep this exercise simple as you are re-training your mind to ignore the physical world in order to access the inner worlds of your mind and consciousness.

Once you have mastered the three exercises above then you can move forward to Exercise 4.

Exercise 4 – Deeper Stages of Meditation:

Once you are familiar with practising the meditation in exercise one. The following exercises offer deeper states of relaxation.

Select a piece of relaxing music, something that will take your mind to a quiet place and help you to relax.

Take yourself into the silence you have created from your meditations with whatever method you have chosen.

Once you are there you are going on a journey of the mind to a much deeper state of relaxation.

Visualise that you are at the top of a beautiful carpeted stairway looking down on 10 steps, to your right there is a hand-rail that you can use if you feel more comfortable as you begin to descend the stairway within your mind's eye.

Taking the steps one at a time, slowly from 10, 9, 8, 7, 6, 5, mind, body and spirit totally relaxed, 4, 3, 2, 1, 0 you can visualise just ahead of you there is a door, you can see that quite clearly within your mind, you now make your way over to the door, open it and enter, closing the door behind you as you go.

You are now in your own very special place, a place you have created within your own mind, a place of beauty, peace and harmony where no one is allowed to enter without your permission.

There is a comfortable chair to sit on, and somewhere comfortable to lie down, just close your eyes and begin to drift a little deeper, and deeper until you are totally relaxed as that being of white light that you really are.

You are aware now of the quiet, relaxing music that you have chosen and you feel in complete harmony within. You are going to remain there, for however long you wish, becoming aware of all you are seeing, hearing, or perhaps just sensing going on all around you, and when you are ready just start very slowly to bring yourself back once more to reality.

As you begin to leave your own very special place, try to remember all that you perceived during your time there.

You are making your way back through the door, carefully closing it behind you and just ahead of you is the stairway, you are now going to make your way back up, starting from 0, 1, 2, 3, 4, 5, mind, body and spirit starting to return to normality, 6, 7, 8, 9, 10 taking your time, you are now back in your own reality, remembering all that happened to you whilst in the state of meditation.

It is a good thing, at this point, to write down a few notes of what you perceived during this altered state as you may use them as reference in the future.

Please bear in mind that whilst in that deeper state of meditation, you are totally in charge of who enters into your mind space, no one can enter without you allowing this to happen.

So please keep in mind the saying "Positive Thoughts Create Positive Things".

It is important to tell you that you cannot come to any harm during these altered states, as you are dealing totally with your own mind, and therefore you hold the power of your own thoughts.

Enjoy the journey.

Psychic Groups

Card Readings

In your development group your tutor will ask you to work in pairs so that one may read the cards of the other person. The tutor may use several different sets of cards, for example, tarot, angel, runes, psy, fairy cards, **or** whatever is available, the reader will then ask the sitter to select a few cards for the reader to work with.

The reader will then begin to focus on these cards and relay what the cards mean to them and connect that to the sitter, you will be quite surprised at the accuracy of the reading.

What in actual fact you are doing as the reader is attuning yourself to sitters vibration by focusing on what cards they have chosen. With practice you will soon become aware of what your own thoughts are and what thoughts you are receiving on a psychic level from the sitter's vibration.

At this stage you are only reading on an inner level, spirit incarnate connected to the physical being. Reading the cards, of course, is a science and you can teach yourself how to do it by studying any deck of cards you feel drawn to learn about. You will very soon realise that not all knowledge is coming from the cards but from your own psyche when you practise focusing your mind.

For all communications to take place on whatever level the use of your mind plays the most important part for your development.

Psychometry:

The art of mentally tuning into the vibrations of an object belonging to someone in your group, perhaps a piece of jewellery, photograph, keys, stones, anything personal. In my case on one instance, placed on the table before me was an artificial leg, of course, for obvious reasons on that occasion I knew right away who I needed to speak with, but really just anything that holds a memory for the person with whom you are working with.

The articles will be placed secretly, whenever possible, on a table in front of the whole group and you as the reader will be asked to select one of them. At this stage you will not know who you will be reading for, as you will be giving off the thoughts that come to you whilst holding the object and tuning into the vibration surrounding it. When you have finished, the information received will be clarified from the person to whom the article belongs.

Colour Exercises:

One of the most popular exercises to be used as it very much relates to the aura and can be used in many different ways both for psychic and mediumistic development.

The group can use coloured ribbons, for instance in reading for each other, the tutor selecting who you work with and placing you together asking that one of you select three different ribbons as the sitter, and the other reading the colours that have been chosen, passing on to the sitter all thoughts that come to you when working with each individual ribbon. At this stage, perhaps what is going on in the sitter's life – health, relationships, finance, work, whatever, very much a psychic connection, really just to clarify to the sitter what is going on around them at this time, when the reader has finished, the sitter can clarify the accuracy of the reading then the role can be reversed.

You may also use colour by just pairing off with someone within the group without ribbons and try to tune into their aura by asking the sitter to think of three colours to pass on to the reader one at a time, whereby the reader will work with the chosen colours, tuning into each vibration bringing forward memories of the past, present, and future.

The sitter will then clarify the information given which is another very good exercise on focusing the mind, and then the roles can be reversed.

Listed here are my interpretations of what thoughts and vibrations the colours bring to my mind, of course as you develop you may perceive them to be different as there are no set rules:

Base Chakra – Red: Opening up to the universal consciousness, psychic awareness, finding the inner self.

Sacral Chakra – Orange: Focused in the moment, needs of a physical nature to be attended to at this time, important issues within your life.

Solar Plexus Chakra – Yellow: Psychic/mediumistic awakening within, searching for answers, a time of learning, both spiritual and physical.

Heart Chakra – Green/Pink: Feelings of emotion, healing and caring for yourself and others.

Throat Chakra – Blue: Communication, important that you say what you feel both spiritually and physically, a need to express oneself. Centre for clairaudience, hearing discarnate beings within the physical body.

Forehead Chakra – Indigo/Purple: Spiritual/psychic awareness, enlightenment to the source, centre for clairvoyance, seeing discarnate beings within your mind's eye.

Crown Chakra – White: – Connecting with discarnate sources, inner and outer vibrations, altered states of consciousness on many levels to reach the real you – The Source.

In the beginning you may use these colours separately but when you become more attuned to them you will realize that all things begin to come together with the sensing of these colours and all vibrations connected within them, then you begin to become aware that you are clairsentient, all methods of communication coming together, therefore embracing all the colours of the chakras on many different levels.

Assometry:

The tutor will ask the group to form a circle, placing in the centre of the circle a chair, then selecting one student as a reader to leave the room for a short period of time and not to return until asked to do so.

The tutor will then ask one of the students to sit on the chair in the centre of the circle for a few moments, and at the same time the sitter will within their own mind send out positive pleasant thoughts, perhaps memories of a happy situation, thereby leaving a nice vibration on the chair for the reader to work with.

The sitter will then return to their seat within the circle, the reader will now be asked to come back into the room and sit on the chair in the centre of the circle for a few moments, trying to link into the vibration of the previous sitter and relaying all thoughts they are receiving at this time to the circle. Without knowing who the sitter is at this point, when the reader has completed all they have perceived the sitter will make them self known and clarify the correctness of the reading.

It is a fun exercise and can be used on a day to day basis. All you have to do is sit in a chair after someone, any place, any time, but please do not relay information to anyone without their permission, or your will be looked upon as being rather naughty, invading privacy, although it is a very good exercise for trying to find out the personality of someone.

I suspect by now you have realised why I call this exercise ass-ometry. – Have fun.

Ouija Board:

There has been over the years a lot of negative thoughts about ouija boards but let me share my experience of the ouija board with you. The board itself is only a word board, used very much as a fun game to create psychic energy, if used for the right purpose then you can have a lot of fun using it. Like all psychic props it is best used with several people at once to create the necessary mind energy to get results, as with all psychic communications there has to be a focus.

The board itself usually comprises of the 26 letters of the alphabet set around the top of the board with the word yes in one corner and no in the other with the numbers 0 – 9 along the bottom, and a wooden pointer, is all you need to receive communication through the board.

It is a rather tedious, time consuming way of communicating psychic energy and requires a lot of patience, so if you have patience then this is what you need to do.

Place the board on a table, or make up your own board, a good number of people using the board at any one time is three and one person to take notes.

You can begin by three sitters placing one finger very gently on the pointer and asking your questions, keeping your questions quite simple in the beginning thereby allowing the energy to build up within the board. At first when the pointer begins to move to the letters of the alphabet and starts to form words, they may seem rather mixed, but that is a natural reaction, as you will have to build up the harmony between the sitters. Just keep writing down the information given from the board and you will eventually see that it will appear to have a structure. You can rotate your sitters and scribe to see if you have any better communications.

When you are all in positive harmony then you may be quite surprised at the information received, good luck, and have fun.

Table Tilting

What is needed in your group for this exercise is a medium sized table, not too heavy to begin with, therefore allowing you to build up the psychic energy within the table for communication to take place.

The tutor will ask at least six students to sit around the table and place their fingertips very gently on top of the table; you will also need another student to take notes of all communications taking place.

One of the sitters will take on the role as spokesperson and begin by encouraging the other sitters to think positive thoughts into the table for the table to tilt, or produce raps and taps once the energy begins to build. This always works best where there is an element of fun involved, laughter is a great source of energy, the sitters will begin to physically feel the table's vibrations through their fingertips.

When this begins to happen, it is always good to encourage the movement of the table by asking the table to move forward or backwards or perhaps rise up on two legs, on some occasions the table may well be dancing around the room, if the energy is strong enough.

The group should set up a code of communications for when you have the table movements, and want to ask some questions, something in the lines of one tilt for no, two for don't know, three for yes, and four for doubtful and so on.

This method of communication is quite often used within a physical circle, as in the beginning it is a great energy builder for that type of phenomena.

There are many, many different ways to develop your psychic ability, you just need to find what suits you best and work with it. – Good luck.

Psychic Experiences

Let me just share one of my earliest psychic experiences I had many, many years ago when I was very young. From a very early age, I knew that there was something different about me, but not sure what it was, I was always aware of other people's feelings and knew instinctively when someone was hurting, both physically and emotionally I seemed to sense that very easily. At that stage in my life I had no idea about psychic phenomena and what that meant.

When I was a teenager I had one really strong psychic feeling which, I suppose was the start of my interest in the psychic worlds. I was 17 or 18 and I sensed within my mind some very strong impressions which I share with you now.

At the time I was dating my then to be husband (Frank) whom I had met at school when I was 13, so I knew him pretty well and of course, very emotionally attached to him.

On a very cold, frosty Scottish autumn evening Frank decided he was going to Glasgow some 50 miles from where we lived to attend a football game.

In those days we did not have mobile phones, indeed very few people had telephones at home, so there was no way that I could contact him that evening.

I awoke next morning still very sure what I had seen in my mind's eye was absolutely real or correct. When Frank telephoned me at work, I was able to tell him he was involved in what might have been a serious car accident at around ten o'clock the previous evening. He was both surprised and shocked as he had not mentioned the accident to anyone. Luckily he emerged from the wreckage unhurt and to this day thinks he may have a guardian angel.

The realities of how clearly I saw that event especially since it involved Frank had me think differently about my direction in life. And so began my study of the psychic worlds. We, as physical beings hold within a great power and when we begin to attune to vibrations on many levels our lives do change.

SECTION 4

Mediumistic Groups

Medium

Clairvoyance

Clairaudience

Clairsentience

Mediumistic Development

Mental mediumship

Altered state of consciousness

Trance mediumship – development of trance

Light trance – overshadowing

Medium trance – communications from discarnate intelligences

MEDIUMISTIC GROUPS

Medium

My interpretation of a medium is one with the ability to receive communications from a discarnate source of intelligence and act as a bridge between the inner and outer worlds on many levels.

For those who feel they are ready to move forward towards mediumship and have a good understanding of the inner psyche, the incarnate consciousness, and are able to connect with others on a psychic level. You can use this skill to become attuned to the discarnate consciousness outer worlds and link with the universal consciousness on a mediumistic level.

Do not consider entering this development unless you are very sure that you are doing it for the right reasons, the desire to help your fellow man, and those in the outer worlds. You take on a great responsibility at this stage and hold within your grasp the ability to change in some cases, very vulnerable people's lives with the information you impart to them, always remember to keep your thoughts POSITIVE whilst working as a medium, as you will be dealing very much with the emotions of others.

Firstly you must find the right group for you and here are a few thoughts on what you need. At this stage it is very important that your group leader is a medium who has the ability to take you that other step. Again you will be invited to join the group for a probationary period, as it is really important there is harmony within the group as it will eventually become a closed development group and not open to the public.

An ideal number for the group can be somewhere between six and eight sitters, as the work you are about to undertake is very much attuning yourself to the outer worlds, discarnate consciousness, in many different ways. Working with the aura will play a very important part at this stage and your group will help you to achieve the necessary vibrations for this to happen, it is a good place to practise with like-minded people.

At this stage you will be dealing with mental mediumship, where all communications are received through the mind of the medium. There are three main categories to mental mediumship:

Clairvoyance – The medium will receive pictures, symbols, images subjectively, through the third eye, just like a television screen in your forehead, how you will begin to work out what these mean and relay the information to the sitter for clarification – relating to the sixth chakra – the forehead.

Clairaudience – The medium will hear communications from the discarnate intelligences subjectively within their mind, a very positive form of mediumship and can be communicated verbally to the sitter, does not need so much working out – relating to the fifth chakra – the throat.

Clairsentience – Is when the medium is working with all three senses coming together, which for the medium, gives a feeling of just knowing what to say and being in-tune with the discarnate intelligences communicating with blocks of thoughts for the sitter. In most cases of mediumship, I think this is the most common as the medium is in tune with all aspects of the psyche, both inner and outer worlds, the whole deal so to speak – relating to the seventh chakra – the crown.

Mediumistic development is very much a trial and error situation and you will only achieve your goals with patience, practice and dedication to work for the discarnate sources who wish to use you as the bridge for the outer worlds.

This development usually does not come overnight and you will be required to do some really hard soul searching until you are confident with the work you are doing, bearing in mind that the outer worlds also have to attune themselves to your vibration for energies to come together.

I would say to you when you get downhearted and believe me you will be at times as that is part of the mediumship development, because it is a very emotional, personal journey, do not give up, and just try another avenue until you find what suits you best. I can tell you that twenty-five years and more down the line I am still searching for ways to make the communications clearer with the outer worlds, but I am not just so hard on myself now, you see old age brings its bonuses.

Enjoy your journey for there is no going back, now that you have attuned yourself on many levels to the very life source of who you are. It really is all worthwhile.

Mediumistic Development

For the development of mediumship I think it is most important that you understand the mechanics of the psychic worlds first and that you are confident about you and who you are before trying to move forward in your development.

That you have tested your ability as a psychic and you are happy with the results, only then are you ready to attune to the discarnate intelligences that wait to work with you.

At this point it is better to approach the development of mediumship with an open mind and not to expect too much in the beginning, as quite often the mediumship you think is best for you is not the one you eventually develop.

It is better to work with all aspects of communication and leave the decision to those who wish to work with you to find out what works best to enable the bridge between the outer and inner worlds to be built, whereby the discarnate sources working with you will be able to confirm survival of the consciousness after the death of the physical body.

The outer worlds have also to build towards all energies coming together and in the beginning that can be rather time consuming, but well worth the patience needed for this development to take place.

A state of trance is the most important thing that is used in the development of mediumship.

The dictionary meaning of trance is "an altered state of consciousness" of which there are many, many levels. Just let me mention a few here and in what context they are used.

Mental Mediumship

As the word implies, communication received from discarnate sources via the medium's mind, i.e. clairvoyance, clairaudience, clairsentience, already explained under Psychic Development, the medium has consciously sent out the thoughts to the awaiting discarnate source from his/her mind and awaits within his/her mind for the communications to be returned thereby able to pass the communications on to the sitter for whom the medium is reading.

Therefore all communications at this time are received mentally through the medium altering his/her thought vibrations.

At the start of this type of mediumistic development it is a good idea to find a circle of approximately eight people for you to sit in. The basis of this circle at the outset will be meditation, to find the many levels of trance.

Your tutor will have their own ideas on the ways of developing that altered state. You may find a variety of exercises involved but you will soon realise what works best for you.

Then it is a matter of practice to build the confidence needed to sustain this type of mediumship, as you may well want to become a public demonstrator of your mediumship.

There are no set rules in any psychic/mediumistic development as you are all individuals and will develop as such.

This initial step will take time and patience to build, as it is the grounding that is required if you wish to move forward into other trance states, for the possible development of trance or physical mediumship, which is a much rarer form of communication and not easily attained.

Altered State of Consciousness:

Three stages are needed for this communication to take place, and are the most common way for discarnate intelligences to impart information to us.

Conveying the communications in the following manner:-

Discarnate consciousness – incarnate consciousness – consciousness.

Discarnate consciousness – communications from those who have departed from their physical body, there are many levels within the discarnate consciousness.

Incarnate consciousness – the real you, the very source of your being, but connected to your physical body for however long you decide you wish to remain on this earth plane until you return to The Source from where you came.

Conscious mind – the part of us which is always alert to what is going on in a physical, mental and emotional way.

There is no need for the medium to be in a deep trance state as the discarnate intelligence does not need to use the unconscious mind, and communication is given in the above way this is called mental mediumship, the medium is fully aware of what is being brought forward through the conscious mind and therefore the medium's mind needs to be alert, rather than resting.

At this stage the medium is working with what is commonly known as clairvoyance, clairaudience, clairsentience, all through the conscious mind.

TRANCE MEDIUMSHIP – DEVELOPMENT OF TRANCE

- **Do You Want To Be A Trance Medium And Why?
  – What is Trance?**

The dictionary meaning is – An unconscious or dazed state.

- **What Is the Purpose of Trance in Relation to Channelling or Mediumship?**

The purpose is the channel or medium can draw close with the discarnate source intelligences at a deeper level through the thought waves. It can take a little time to build up the necessary vibrations for this to happen, just like fine tuning a radio receiver, all things will come together through the channel/medium being in a relaxed state of mind, so that he/she will be more receptive to receiving the thoughts communicated to them. When we relax the mind then we can begin to go to a deeper level of consciousness for the communications to take place. There are many who wait to make communication in many different ways, as they also have been developing this passive state to make this possible.

The state of deep trance is to help the communicating intelligences get across their messages in a positive way to help mankind go forward, whether that be through channelling/mental/physical mediumship.

- **When Would You Use Trance?**

In all aspects of channelling/mediumship.

- **Do You Know Yourself Sufficiently To Become A Trance Channel/Medium?**

For example: – Who you really are, and the power you hold within you?

- **How Do You Attain The Trance State?**

Through meditation and dedication.

- **What Are the Levels of Trance (consciousness)?**

All levels – depending upon the channel/medium, and where they are in their development.

- **Can You Be Taught Trance?**

Yes – we can all be taught to reach an altered state of consciousness on many levels.

- **What Is The Most Important Thing We Use In The Development Of Trance?**

The mind.

- **What Should Be Uppermost In Our Thoughts For This Channelling To Take Place?**

Getting to know and trust the intelligences who wish to work through your mind and not to be afraid.

Keep an open mind and only accept what feels to be the best, and therefore right for you.

In the beginning always look for the logical answers before you label anything paranormal.

Remain with your feet firmly on the ground.

Light Trance – Overshadowing.

Let me begin by sharing my experiences of the altered states of trance firstly by dealing with what is called overshadowing which means that the medium is in an altered state of consciousness by whichever method he/she has chosen to work with through the meditation processes previously practised until he/she finds what is comfortable.

Once in that required altered state he/she will become aware within their mind that there are incarnate communications being given to them to pass forward, usually at this early stage it comes as inspirational speaking, as the medium is fully aware of what is being said and actively taking part within the communications. The incarnate intelligence is using at this point the medium's altered state of mind to bring forward the information, very often spiritual philosophy or guidance.

In most cases, at this stage the communications are coming from the incarnate intelligence of the medium, in other words the medium's own spirit or thoughts. A very good way of building the confidence needed for the deeper trance states that you might wish to develop.

After working with this type of overshadowing for some time, and you are comfortable with it, you can then begin to move into the next stages of trance development.

Medium Trance – Communications from Discarnate Intelligences.

Now we are moving forward into a deeper state of trance and this type of mediumship, at least in the beginning should be done in a private circle until the medium is confident enough to share the communications on a more public level.

A good idea would be to set up a home circle with a few like minded people, whom you trust and feel confident to sit with, who are willing to give up their time to sit in a circle for the development of the trance medium.

It is always helpful where possible to have a medium who knows the workings of the psychic worlds present at the circle to help the sitters understand what is being brought forward through the trance medium, and of course to take notes and act as a scribe for the circle, as the entranced medium always likes to know what has been going on when returning from the altered states of consciousness.

That does not mean that the trance medium leaves the physical body and allows discarnate intelligences to use it, you as the trance medium are always in control of what happens both physically and mentally, as once again, you are fully aware of what is being said, and the only thing being used at this stage is the medium's mind, but you are a little less in control of what is being said and generally just go with the flow of things, but always in a positive way.

As the development group moves forward, the trance medium will become aware of the many sensations taking place around him/her. In the beginning a feeling of heaviness of the physical body, perhaps a sense of being unable to move, which of course you can if you wish, is only the medium becoming aware of the psychic energies surrounding the sitters and the medium, the outer and inner worlds trying to come together for the communications to take place.

At this early stage it is quite common for discarnate loved ones to use the trance medium whilst in this altered state to bring forward communications for the sitters within the circle, e.g. family, friends, spiritual workers and of course, not forgetting the animals, demonstrating that consciousness lives on after the death of the physical body, paving the way for further development of discarnate intelligences to come forward in a more public demonstration, when the medium has built the confidence and is ready to move forward.

In most cases the sitter will readily recognise the discarnate intelligence immediately by the personality being given, or the mannerisms of the medium changing and taking on the persona of the communicating intelligence.

You may find within your home circle this level of trance is very much used in bringing forward spiritual guidance at a much deeper level and with some mediums having the ability to bring forward guidance from evolved spiritual teachers, to enhance and help our material world, as the evidence is given to the circle as a general reading and not one to one.

Again, I must remind you that there are no set rules in any development, all sittings are very much experimental, and we just never know what is going to come about when we open ourselves up to the psychic worlds, so be ready to be amazed.

Now, if you feel you are ready let us go on to talk of physical mediumship and the many forms relating to that vast subject.

SECTION 5

Deep Trance

Physical phenomena

Apports and asports

Materialization – ectoplasm

Altered state of consciousness

DEEP TRANCE – PHYSICAL PHENOMENA

By far the most controversial subject to be discussed and it is here that I will share my own personal experiences of what happened in my private home circle.

This type of mediumship should most definitely be done in a private circle, a good idea is a home circle, because the medium involved will be in a very much deeper altered state of consciousness and the conditions must be conducive for the physical phenomena to take place.

Many years ago, I myself sat as the developing deep trance medium for physical phenomena, so I would just like to share with you my experiences and those of the circle.

However, I must add although my home circle sat for almost six years, we never did achieve ectoplasm, spiritual energy for the discarnate intelligences to use for communications. However, we did manage to achieve a few other things.

The circle started off with a few dedicated sitters, Anna, Ruby, Frances, Marion, Bill, Betty and on occasions invited guests my husband, family, friends and of course myself, sitting on a very regular basis once a week for approximately two to three hours to try and make communications of a physical nature with discarnate intelligences.

In the early days we sat in silence for meditation, later adding music to allow our thoughts to blend within the circle. We continued in this way until we became attuned to the vibrations, each of us sensing, seeing, hearing different things, but always on a psychic level, within our own minds.

We were all aware of the many changes in temperature and vibrations within the room and what appeared to be cool breezes, feelings of density and in some cases a heaviness within the room.

After the sitting we would discuss what we felt had happened to each of us individually, and jointly, keeping notes of all circle meetings.

The circle decided that we would set up a cabinet for the medium, myself, to sit in to try and enhance the mediumship, as at that point we were having communications through trance speaking.

It is fairly common in physical circles to use a cabinet, the purpose being, the cabinet is a focus point for the sitters to concentrate their thoughts upon, whilst the medium is sitting within the cabinet in an altered state of consciousness, inviting discarnate intelligences to come and join the circle.

In the past most physical circles would be set up in a darkened room, with a few articles taped with luminous tape placed on the floor or table so that they would be easily seen if there was any movement taking place. Articles such as a trumpet, child's toy, flowers, crystals, camera, writing paper and pencil in the hope that the communicators would leave written messages. The objects used were easily moved to allow the sitters to see any movement and demonstrate that physical phenomena was taking place.

Apports and Asports

It is quite common in physical circles to receive what are known as apports into the circle.

Apports are objects which are brought to the circle and left as presents, quite often when the circle is over you will find these articles somewhere in the room. It is my understanding that these articles are dematerialised from another source, on the earth plane, of course, not stolen just attained and materialised into the circle. How cool is that – pretty amazing?

Asports are objects which are taken from the circle and usually never seen again in that circle. I think they may well end up as apports in other circles.

These apported and asported articles can in some cases be old foreign coins, teaspoons, jewellery, photographs, flowers, stones, money whatever, usually small objects but quite often memorabilia.

But for some strange reason, in my own circle it works in the reverse from the normal procedure of firstly receiving apports, as my experiences have been that the same object is asported, taken from the circle and apported, brought back into the circle at a later date.

So no presents for me, to date, just borrowing what belongs to me, and returning them at a much later date, but that is okay because I like things to be a little different, and I think perhaps I am dealing with discarnate intelligences who have a sense of humour.

Below are a few examples of what has happened in my home circle.

After sitting for several years and not getting what I hoped to achieve, physical phenomena, I was becoming quite frustrated, after all I was the trance medium, and felt that I was letting my circle down, which in actual fact was absolutely silly, as you cannot demand anything from anyone, never mind trying to get physical contact from a discarnate source. Although I was very appreciative of what was happening within the circle, like all humans I want more.

One evening while meditating alone I sent a very positive thought to the discarnate intelligences who work with me asking that I be given some proof that physical phenomena is possible. I wanted it to be something I was really sure did happen, never thinking for a moment it would, but ever hopeful.

Several weeks went by, the circle met as usual, and I had not mentioned to anyone what I had actually asked for.

Shortly afterwards my husband and I went off for the weekend with some friends. I took two gold necklaces which were special gifts from my husband, and since I cherish them, I am always careful where and when I wear them.

We returned from the weekend and my circle met a few days later. The morning after, I asked my husband what he had done with my necklaces as I distinctly remember laying them on the mantelshelf (in the room where the circle was held) but they were no longer there.

My husband thought I had left them behind in the hotel. I did telephone without success, besides I was certain where I had left them.

Approximately three months later I returned from work and was preparing to go to a local church to take a service of clairvoyance. Earlier that day I had given a thought as to what had happened to my necklaces.

I went into my jewellery wrap (although I had previously checked it) and to my amazement the gold necklaces dropped out, in absolutely pristine condition.

Just then I heard my husband come in, I ran downstairs to show him the necklaces. I was further surprised to learn from him that he too had been thinking about the necklaces and at lunch time that day had decided to remove the mantelshelf in case they had fallen behind, alas no success.

In our minds there is absolutely no doubt that the psychic worlds proved physical phenomena on that occasion in a very positive way that we will most certainly remember, and of course appreciate the efforts of the discarnate intelligences involved in doing so. They most certainly gave us something to think about.

Sadly, after almost six years the circle had to be closed as my husband and I moved house and it was a few years later that we decided to start another circle.

When looking back and reflecting upon all the things that did happen in that circle I am pleased to say that there was so much psychic development went on both on a physical and emotional level, most of the sitters went on to become working mediums in many different aspects of the paranormal.

So you see, the discarnate intelligences never waste our time, that they will use whatever is possible for the further advancement of their work in whatever way they can to bring about a better understanding that life is eternal.

Everything is about the joy we feel whilst sitting to connect to The Source of all being in whatever way we can, in trying to find the best within ourselves to share with one another, whether that be as a psychic/medium/channel on any level.

* * *

Let me now share with you our latest experience of the paranormal now that Frank and I have moved and we are settled.

We decided we would set up a home circle once again, just the two of us in the beginning to see what might transpire. We sit every Sunday evening for approximately one hour.

We did not have to wait too long for physical activity to take place, let me just share this experience with you – The case of the missing cooking oil.

We had been sitting once a week for several months, just enjoying the peace and blending with the discarnate intelligences with all the usual psychic happenings going on, changes in temperature, cracking noises within the room, feeling of heaviness in the atmosphere, just generally attuning ourselves to the outer worlds in the hope that we may receive physical phenomena.

I decided that I would send a thought out to the discarnate intelligences that work with me, of which Frank was not aware, to ask if it was possible, that we could achieve physical phenomena in time. You have probably guessed by now that I do not always, sadly, have great patience.

The following transpired:-

My husband Frank and I were shopping and bought a litre bottle of cooking oil. I used some the same evening and afterwards put it in the kitchen cupboard. The following morning I went to use the oil again and found it had disappeared. I searched everywhere in the kitchen in case I had mislaid it – without success.

My husband suggested perhaps I had thrown it out with the rubbish. I checked the bin and again had no luck; my husband checked the car although he knew I had used the oil.

The next week I was in Spain for a few days' spiritual work and workshops, my husband was away from home at the same time. We got back on a Sunday which is when we sit in the home circle, and when I opened the kitchen cupboard, there, right in the middle of the shelf was the cooking oil, less of course what we had previously used before it disappeared.

I am in no doubt that the oil was moved from the kitchen and returned at a later date, fascinating, and I am certain that I have communication going on in a physical way by taking articles from my home and returning them some time later, I look forward with anticipation to any other physical phenomena taking place

The latest experience is I have a very favourite vegetable knife, which I have had for many years and I have taken from house to house with me, surprise, surprise, it has gone missing.

Now, because I am a very logical person, I will look at the logical answer first, that being, have I thrown it out with the vegetable peelings, or has it just gone missing, to be returned at a later date.

Only time will tell, but I must emphasise at this stage how important it is when sitting for physical phenomena that you keep yourself grounded and always look for the logical answers first, as in most cases, there usually are simple answers.

However, I am in absolutely no doubt that it is possible under certain conditions to achieve physical communications from discarnate intelligences and when that phenomena is achieved we are truly privileged to be a part of that happening.

Good luck with your development keep your thoughts positive and strive for the best you can achieve.

Materializations – Ectoplasm:

I fully understand the deepest altered state of consciousness is needed for these phenomena to take place. However, I do have my own thoughts and how it is achieved, but I will share them with you at the end of this section.

At this stage I will give you my personal views on this type of mediumship, as in my twenty five years of studying the paranormal I have not as yet had the privilege of witnessing full materialization through ectoplasm, but I am open to offers.

There are of course, some excellent examples on the internet which you can readily view. But for me I need to see the real thing, as I have already mentioned, I am a very logical person and it is very important that I am absolutely certain of what I am witnessing in a physical way, with my own eyes, before I can label anything paranormal out of respect for the discarnate intelligences who work with me, as this is a very misunderstood form of mediumship.

When the deep trance medium/channel sits for this type of phenomena it is most certainly done under very controlled circumstances, in the beginning, most definitely in a private circle as the medium is in a very vulnerable state and totally dependent upon the circle leader and the sitters to maintain the correct ambience for the phenomena to take place.

In a materialization sitting, what is anticipated to happen is that the medium will go into the altered state of consciousness needed to bring forward the discarnate intelligences i.e. family, friends, helpers, loved ones to communicate in a physical way with the sitters.

As the word implies materialization when all present at the sitting should see the same thing, at the same time, with the physical eyes then there is absolutely no doubt that everyone is witnessing the same phenomena, and there is no question it could be clairvoyance, as different sitters may perceive different phenomena psychically, if indeed that happens, then of course, the communications cannot be described as physical.

Ectoplasm is the substance used in the materializing of the communicating discarnate intelligence. I believe at this time, no one really knows what that substance is made from, it has been tested scientifically and no definite conclusions found, to date, and sadly that does make it difficult to replicate the substance, as the sample piece used disintegrated within a few days.

When the medium/channel brings forward the ectoplasm whilst in a deep trance state, it usually emanates from the medium's orifices, nose, mouth and the solar plexus.

The ectoplasm has been described as a gauze like material, which starts to form very slowly into a discarnate communicator, who can be seen as a solid mass, by everyone in the circle, and having the ability in some cases, to communicate in a physical way, by speaking and touching their loved ones here on the earth plane whilst in the materialized form – wow, that would be something to see, how marvellous.

When the communications are over the ectoplasm dematerializes by returning once again back into the entranced medium through the orifices. The medium will then start to bring their consciousness back within their physical body thereby returning from the deep trance state.

If the channel's incarnate consciousness has the ability to hold the thoughts of the discarnate intelligence then you will have materialization, physical phenomena.

There is no way, sadly, at this time that any scientist would accept that as truth, that is why I say to you, it is my interpretation of what appears to be happening at this moment. Of course you may know different, in which case, good luck with your search.

I believe that there are a few mediums/channels here on this earth plane today who have developed the ability to achieve physical phenomena, materialization, ectoplasm through becoming attuned to their own incarnate consciousness to receive these communications they are usually people who have sat for many years in development with the inner and outer psychic worlds.

There are those chosen few who come to this earth plane already developed and willing to share with us the truths of the outer psychic worlds when we are ready to listen.

This is only a brief review of physical mediumship covering ectoplasm, as that is what I am most interested in at this moment. There are other types of phenomena being achieved under the umbrella of physical communication without ectoplasm which of course needs to be discussed with a totally different approach.

As we in the material world move forward in a more technical way in our search for answers to the paranormal, there are many ways available in which to research for the truths you are seeking, let me just list a few of these below, all of which you can research on the internet:-

Digital Recordings

Computers – Communications.
Photography.
E.V.P. – Electronic Voice Phenomena.
Direct Voice.

I am sure there are many, many more technical aids available to us in our search, all of which have a purpose and are most definitely of value in trying to bridge the gap between the inner and outer worlds. Communication can be proved in a more scientific way, all of which do not need to use ectoplasm.

But, I must finish this section by saying at this time without a deep trance medium you would not be able to attain ectoplasm for the materializations and the physical contact between the two worlds, which again brings me back to my thinking that the ectoplasm is indeed. – Thought forms transferred into solid mass.

I am in no doubt whatsoever that in time we can achieve contact with the outer worlds, in a more physical way with the dedication and hard work of those of us who are willing to spend our time in researching the many avenues available.

Altered State of Consciousness:

Conveying the deep trance state, commonly used in physical communications.

Four stages are needed for deep trance state to be achieved:-

Discarnate consciousness, incarnate consciousness, unconscious, conscious mind.

Discarnate consciousness – communications from those who have departed from their physical body, there are many levels within the discarnate consciousness.

Incarnate consciousness – the real you, the very source of your being, but connected to your physical body for however long you decide you wish to remain on this earth plane until you return to The Source from where you came.

Unconscious – commonly know as the sub-conscious and is part of the mind which lies deep within our consciousness, the part that holds all our memories past, present and future.

Conscious mind – the part of us which is always alert to what is going on in a physical, mental and emotional way.

The medium placing them self into an altered state of consciousness i.e. sleep state through – meditation, anaesthesia, hypnosis, allowing the conscious mind into a state of rest, (altered state). This would make sense of the medium saying when they come back from the altered state that they have no recall whilst in that state of consciousness. Indeed they are most likely in sleep state and the discarnate source is able to use the unconscious mind for the communications to take place.

The discarnate intelligence can then impart communications through the incarnate consciousness to the unconscious mind of the medium and finally to the voice box of the medium to relay the vocal communications, or through the medium's orifices when ectoplasm is being used.

It is my belief that if the medium is totally attuned with the discarnate consciousness then it is possible to produce ectoplasm. I believe the ectoplasm to be formed thoughts from the discarnate intelligence and transmitted through the incarnate to the unconscious mind of the medium then the medium transmits these thoughts into solid mass (ectoplasm) for physical phenomena to take place, but, of course I have no way of proving that – I only know that it all makes sense to me if the medium's altered states of consciousness are in tune with the discarnate consciousness then things will happen.

SECTION 6

Amusing happenings

From The Source – Be happy

AMUSING HAPPENINGS

As you can well imagine over twenty five years of paranormal research I have heard a few funny stories in my time, which relate to what I do as a psychic/medium, so let me just share a few with you.

No matter where you go in this world you will always find the cynic, to which of course, I have no objections, as I believe the more people asking questions of the workings of the psychic worlds, the more knowledge we will gain.

What does upset me is the sceptic who is critical before asking the questions. I do like a good discussion and I am always open to the point of view of others.

I was enjoying a bar-b-que one evening with some friends and was introduced to a young man and his family. He was very friendly till someone mentioned I was a psychic medium. His attitude changed completely. I became the devil incarnate and should be burnt at the stake. I could not believe we still have people so biased and so conditioned. He then told me his father died recently and I should be able to tell him his father's name.

His negative taunts upset me so I asked, "Why ask the question. Don't you know your father's name?" I met him some time later and we became good friends. He was by no means a stupid young man, only a misguided one.

***

Together with a friend I took a demonstration of mediumship in a local town hall.

The hall seated about fifty people and was rather busy. The evening started well with communications being accepted. My colleague asked a gentleman in the audience if she could speak with him – he replied. "Certainly".

The communication was from his wife giving her personal details and of how close she is to him. When my colleague asked him to clarify if the communication was correct, he looked somewhat puzzled and answered. "The message can't be for me, my wife died a few years ago."

It was then explained to him he was attending a demonstration of clairvoyance.

He replied, "I was out for a walk, noticed the crowd entering the hall and thought I'd join them especially since it was free".

It is extraordinary that when the discarnate communicators wish to speak with someone they find the means to do so.

After the meeting the gentleman said he was pleased he had unwittingly attended the meeting and the message he received from his wife was correct.

***

Another medium friend of mine told me his story of one demonstration:-

He went to a lady in the congregation and asked if he could speak with her. She very cheerfully replied, "Yes", my friend went on to say, "I have your husband coming forward who wishes to speak with you".

The lady replied, "Well you can keep him. He did not speak to me when he was alive, so I am not going to speak to him just because he is dead".

You can imagine how my friend felt. There was nothing he could do except join in the laughter. On that occasion he was unable to pass on the message.

***

I was asked by a medium friend if I would help with a charity evening of clairvoyance in aid of a children's charity.

"Of course", I willingly said, "It would be a pleasure". The evening was held in the church where I am a tutor/demonstrator so a lot of my students were present. The church was packed to capacity. There were a few mediums working the platform and, the evening was going well, with each medium taking a turn to demonstrate.

When it came to my turn, I went right to the back of the church and asked the lady in the back row if I could speak with her. She replied "Definitely not. I do not want a message".

You could feel the tension within the church and the gasps around the room. There I was with a somewhat dented ego, having to think very quickly how to get out of this dilemma. No one had prepared me for such a response.

Strangely, I went on to speak with another lady on the opposite side of the church, giving her the next communication, surprise, surprise. I was talking to the first lady's sister who told me who she was when I finished giving her the messages.

A lot of information given related to the sister who had refused to accept the communication.

With a smile I said to the first lady "You see, my dear, you did not want to speak to your loved ones but they really wanted to speak to you and their message was relayed to you by speaking with your sister."

The discarnate intelligences with whom we work also have a sense of humour.

***

My local church invited a trance medium to give demonstrations of clairvoyance and trance mediumship.

The medium worked over two evenings and although we had never met, I was invited to chair for her on the first evening of clairvoyance.

As I was about to leave for the venue, my husband said he would like to attend the meeting. He is very supportive of my work but he does not usually take an active part.

I explained we should enter the church separately (I already knew he was going to receive a message) in case any reference was made that might link us.

The meeting started and was going very well, the communications all being accepted. The medium then said she wanted to speak to the gentleman in the front row; it was, of course, my husband.

She gave him some excellent information, all of which I perfectly understood but his replies were mostly non-committal although I could see he was a little shocked and more than a little surprised.

After the meeting my husband asked me to answer his many questions.

On the second evening I attended the trance demonstration alone and I received a communication from the medium whilst she was in an entranced state, from her guide who said he was an Irish peddler called Michael.

The message went something like this; "I want to speak with the lady near the front whose name is Beatrice".

I was the only Beatrice there – "Yes certainly" I said. He said "I have a message for the gentleman who calls you Beatty".

The communicator said he was in our house the previous evening, listening to my husband bombarding me with questions. However I was not to worry as Michael was going to arrange a little visit for him, to clarify he is real and what he said the evening before is real also.

As time passes experiences are put to the back of your mind and stored there until something occurs which jogs the memory.

We were watching television one evening and as he was feeling tired, decided to go upstairs to bed. About fifteen minutes later there was such a commotion coming from upstairs I thought my husband had fallen out of bed. Then suddenly the lounge door was thrown open and he rushed in, obviously deeply distressed, clutching his chest. I thought he must be seriously ill but once I calmed him down he said.

"I was drifting off to sleep when I became aware of a man standing by the bedside. Although I could not describe his appearance, I knew it was a man who appeared to be holding me down. I remember thinking is this the visit I was told about?"

I found my husband's reaction to the visit highly amusing, the thought of him being so scared of something he really didn't believe in. He quickly recovered and is now very respectful of the psychic worlds.

Which proves to me, when the discarnate intelligences who work with us wish to make themselves known then there is no way that we can stop them.

Now, when the unexpected happens around him, he very quickly gives me a shout to help him understand what is going on.

***

From The Source – Be Happy

Joy is the very nature of your creation, it is one of the greatest vibrations humans have, the one which brings happiness into your life. When you understand that it is your right to be joyful then many things will change.

Try not to focus too much on the past and stay focused in the now, appreciate who you are and those around daily, all life is a gift, to be cherished and enjoyed.

You are a being of light and as such it is your right to shine that light whenever you have the opportunity, as people will be drawn to you and the light within you. There is no need to be serious as all things can be achieved with laughter. What you can be is seriously happy which is different from being just happy.

Do not punish yourself by asking for what you think are impossible things to achieve by yourself. Nothing is impossible; it is only your attitude that stops your desires from happening. You must remember the law of attraction which is a universal law and related to your thoughts and intentions whether they are good or bad, so be very careful how you think as you might just get what you ask for.

Most of the time human beings just keep running around chasing their tails, like the never-ending circle of life, that is because you focus your intentions upon this material world and not the outer world where all questions can be, and are, answered when you become attuned to that source.

The question that goes on, and on, and on, and on, is of course "Is There Life after Death?" when in fact the statement should be "There Is No Death". When you start to make that statement, then you are on your way to understanding the secrets of the universe itself, which, really are not secrets, you have just been searching in the wrong direction.

Once you bring yourself into alignment with The Source then your whole perspective of life changes for a much happier and fulfilled life on this earthly vibration.

Open the doors of your mind and let the joy flow in.

SECTION 7

Paranormal Research.

Introduction to paranormal researchers – November 2007.

Paranormal experiment – February 2008.

Testimonials of two paranormal researchers involved in February 2008 experiment.

Invitation from Edinburgh Society of Psychical Research – Experimental

Evening on 2nd December 2008.

Experimental psychic evening – 2nd December 2008.

Testimonial for December experiment.

PARANORMAL RESEARCH

Introduction to Paranormal Researchers – November 2007.

In November 2007, I was approached by Archibald A. Lawrie a well known, respected, psychic researcher who heard I am able to demonstrate paranormal communications from a discarnate source of intelligence on a regular basis, sometimes before the event takes place. I have spent many years demonstrating mediumship and receiving communications – in some cases several weeks before the event has occurred. I have attended meetings, on occasions, with my notebook containing messages from my contacts and simply read them out.

I accepted the invitation offered to carry out the experiment for the progress of all things paranormal as there is no doubt in my mind there is a far greater universal intelligence waiting to work with us.

Between 6th December 2007 and 21st January 2008, the communications were given to me via my mind telling me about the venue for the experiment. I had no knowledge where it was to be, or indeed who would be there, as that was left to the researchers to arrange. I only attended on the night of the experiment.

I was told previously by discarnate energies who would receive the communications, where they would be sitting and what they would be wearing. These details were sent to the Psychic Researcher on different dates, whereby they were placed safely in a signed, sealed envelope and given to a Solicitor to lock away in his safe, and only brought out on the night of the Experiment 24th February 2008.

Preparations for the experiment were completed by 21st January and locked away. Invitations were sent to 25 people on 27th January. Therefore the communications were written before the recipients of the messages knew they were being invited to take part.

The result was impressive although not perfect. When dealing with a discarnate consciousness who is trying to convey information through my mind, that information may become slightly distorted as all energies have to merge for it to happen.

I feel this work requires further investigation, much praise and credit to the discarnate energies.

PARANORMAL EXPERIMENT FEBRUARY 2008

Thursday 6th December 2007 – 10:22a.m. – Sitting for communication from "The Others".

I am asking to be shown the venue for February and I am receiving the following information:-

I am aware of standing outside a house and ahead there is a slightly elevated pathway leading to a rather large front door. On either side of the path is a garden area and the house is attached to another on the right. I enter the house, through a small hall which has a tiled floor, move forward through an inner door where there is a room to the right and one to the left beyond which there is a staircase leading to an upstairs area. There are also flowers in the hall on the right. It is conveyed to me that the communications will take place in the room on the right. I enter the room through a fairly large door and I am facing a window, there is also a fireplace on the left. I feel the room is used as a study as there are lots of books with a bookcase behind.

I can only describe this room as being very welcoming and I am aware of other energy sources already present. I sense too, a strong vibration of knowledge.

Standing in the room with my back to the window I am conscious it is from this point that I have to work. Before starting the communications I feel a strong urge to say the numbers 3 and 7 which are being given to me. I don't understand their relevance at this time but I know it will later become clear.

Thursday 6th December 2007 – 10:22a.m. – Sitting for communication from "The Others".

1. **I am being shown that the first lady with whom I will speak is on my right side, I want to laugh because I think "The Others" are playing a joke on me as I am being shown a lady wearing a hat (which is quite unusual in this day) she is very precise in her thinking she also likes to make the best of her appearance and I feel she is a comfortable lady well rounded but looks rather stern, I feel she would have lots of questions for us, as she is no stranger to this type of research.**

I feel I have a lady coming forward for her who tells me she is her mother, I feel the lady to be of a very strong character as she draws close with her daughter she has come to tell her that the thoughts she has been sending are true and wants you to know that you are doing the right thing she will be there to support you, she also brings forward with her your father who stands behind her at this time in a supportive way and says "you see nothing changes she is still in charge" I feel him to be a very gentle soul and is around you when you most need him. I also feel the name of John is relevant in this communication, as there is a closeness with him and he wants you to know that all is well (although you know this already). As I start to draw away from you I now hear brother being called in to be remembered to you. I will leave you now take their love and know they are only a thought away. Don't forget about Mary.

Wednesday 12th December – 12.25 a.m. – Experimental sitting for communications from "The Others."

2.   Left hand side towards the middle – Lady with dark hair, wearing glasses who would understand the name of Mary being called in. I feel the lady is wearing black/white around her shoulders.

I feel I have a gentleman coming forward at this time and I am hearing the name of Joe being called in. I feel that I have a father coming forward now who wants to link to his daughter. I am aware of lots of emotion with this communication, tears from him and you. He says you must keep your chin up for you know the work has to be done. I am hearing mother being called in now and I am aware of a lady coming forward for you, just to support you at this time. The February month is important for you (many changes) the name of Elizabeth is being given to you and I am hearing that your daughter will be well. I am being shown a small dog for you as a memory of better times.

Take the love of the spirit people and know that they are around you in your time of need.

Wednesday 12th December – 12.25 a.m. – Experimental sitting for communications from "The Others."

3.   Left hand side near front – Lady rather rounded – the colour red around her also wearing black beads, she is here with a friend although she is rather sceptical but willing to listen.

I have a lady coming forward and I feel she is your mother. I feel she has not done anything like this before and is trying her best to communicate with you, she says lighten up and let it happen. I feel the lady to have a great personality and liked to laugh but says you are not finding a lot to laugh about so far and she wants you to try and put the smile back on your face. She is calling the name "James or Jim or perhaps both". I am not too sure on that one but hopefully you will understand. She is talking of a move of home for you at this time and gives you the go ahead. I feel father also wants to be remembered to you as he comes forward he says just for support as you need reassurance at this time. I am hearing the name of Tom being called in and also hearing brother must link with that name. I am aware of a gentleman now who tells me he passed very quickly (heart attack) who is very close to you (partner perhaps!!) but says he is fine now the month of February is an anniversary time of a passing and lots of nice thoughts connect to that. As I leave you I am aware of a black cat wandering about your feet and I feel that is a memory for you.

Lots of love from.

R. and P.

Wednesday 12th December – 12.25 a.m. – Experimental sitting for communications from "The Others."

4.   **Right hand side of room – Lady/gentleman sitting together, I can see a walking stick between them, I feel the gentleman would need to use it.**

I feel I have both mother and father coming forward for the gentleman as your health has not been good at this time and they are trying to comfort you and help you to come to terms with things and assuring you that you can cope to take the strength of the lady with you and not to be so stubborn. They also want to thank the lady very much for taking care of their son and they say you are like a daughter to them. I am hearing the name of Mary being called in for you as she draws very close to be remembered to you.

Love to the boys (grandchildren).

Monday 21st January 2008, 20:10 – Experimental sitting for communication from "The Others".

5.   **Left hand side near back row gentleman on his own wearing a suit (grey) collar and tie. Researcher but he is a bit sceptical at this time. You also have a watch which belonged to your father.**

I feel I have a father coming forward for you, he tells me you are very like him, that you have a very inquisitive mind and are constantly searching for answers to many things – life being one of them. He says you become rather frustrated with your work at times and it is important that you continue with your latest project, he says he will be able to assist you by inspiring you to write more. I am hearing the name of Tom being called in for you but I feel that to be a friendship link and he tells me there was much fun with you both. I also have mother coming forward and I can see a rather well dressed lady with white/grey hair, she would have been a very proud lady whilst here on the earth plane but she needs you to know that she was always proud of you. She says your aunt is also with her and wants to be remembered to you. I feel that has something to do with playing a piano (either her or both of you) but she says you will understand that. The two ladies make me aware that you have been having a slight problem with your chest and it is really important that you do what the doctor advises and do not overlook the medication. Try not to burn the candle at both ends. Take the love of those who watch over you.

The initials "W" and "J" are relevant as communicators. (Love to brother).

Monday 21ˢᵗ January 2008, 20:10 – Experimental sitting for communication from "The Others".

6. **Near to front row (perhaps left hand side) – lady sitting near end of a row – darkish hair wearing glasses looks like something white around her neck or (something lacy) also wearing a chain with a cross or pendant around her neck.**

I am hearing the name of Mary being called in quite strongly and you would understand that. I am also being told there is a lady here who would have passed after a cancerous illness and I feel that to be in the breast and chest areas, she wishes to draw close to you, just to say she is alright now and a very big thank you. I am also aware of a lady who is very strong of character and hearing mother being called in for you, I feel the lady is rather rounded and very neat in her appearance, also her personality to be rather strict but nice, I just know I would not be answering her back. I am hearing the name of Elizabeth being called in also for you and that the January month is an important time to you (an anniversary) of a gentleman who would have passed then and I feel him to be family, he says he passed quickly and pain free as his last memory is finding himself in a new dimension in which he is very comfortable.

He says thank you for talking to the picture so often and that he receives your thoughts and sends all his love, also to the two boys.

Monday 21st January 2008, 20:10 – Experimental sitting for communication from "The Others".

7.   Left hand side about 4th row from front somewhere in the middle of a row – lady wearing a dark coat with a coloured scarf around her neck. A lot of emotion around this lady at this time as I can see the colour green around her.

I am being told that there is a lot of healing being sent to you at this time as you have been rather ill. It is important that you know that things will much improve over the next six months, that a change of treatment will be offered to which you must agree to. Your loved ones draw very close with you at this time and are trying to lift your spirit as that is very important for you to receive the necessary help. I am hearing the name of William being called in also I have a father coming forward for you, he says someone to lean on and to support you. He is talking of the April month and says "happy birthday". Love to my granddaughter. He tells me I must move away from you now as you will not be able to cope with the emotion and he will contact you again in the near future. Take his love and know that he is with you always, he is putting the initial "J" over your head and that is meant for someone here on the earthly vibration where he also wishes to be remembered.

Communications Completed

Testimonials of the two Paranormal Researchers involved in the February 2008 Experiment.

"Commendation
As a professional psychical researcher over the years, as someone who is Vice-president of The Scottish Society of Psychical Research and Founder of The Edinburgh Society for Psychical Research, I am privileged to meet and work with some of Scotland's finest mediums.

I wish that I had met Beatrice years before now, for some of her beliefs regarding the working mechanisms of the psychic world are very close to my own, while her undoubted talents do her great credit.

Archibald A. Lawrie,
Author, Broadcaster, Advisor to the BBC and Film-making Groups worldwide.

Beatrice is a talented and experienced Medium. She has had lengthy experience of working both in the UK and abroad. She is a committed and active member of her profession not only in conducting Public Demonstrations and Private Sittings but also in her Tutoring; where she ensuring her students receive a thorough and intensive grounding in all aspects of Psychic Development. As well as this, she possesses an unusual talent for being able to receive 'messages' from spirit well in advance of any meeting taking place. She knows who the message if for and where they will be sitting in the meeting hall – even before the person themselves know whether they will be attending or not!

This unusual talent for Pre-cognition has been tested independently where her marks for accuracy have consistently scored around 80%!

This is a medium with a vast knowledge and experience to draw from and one from which a lot can be learnt. It has been a pleasure and privilege to know and work with Beatrice and I'm pleased to be able to call her my friend.

Ann Treherne
Psychic Researcher.

Invitation from Edinburgh Society for Psychical Research -

Experimental Evening on 2nd December 2008.

In the month of July 2008 I was approached once again by Archie A. Lawrie, professional psychical researcher, President of The Edinburgh Society for Psychical Research and Vice-President of the Scottish Society for Psychical Research who asked me if I would be willing to participate in another experimental evening with the society.

The experimental evening took place on 2nd December 2008 at 246 Morrison Street, Edinburgh, where this experiment was open to the public.

The following transpired, and was a very successful Experiment.

EXPERIMENTAL PSYCHIC EVENING
2ND DECEMBER 2008

246 Morrison Street,
Edinburgh.

First Sitting: – 09.30. a.m. Saturday 16th August
2008 to receive communication from Source Energy.
(Sitting taking place at home) for demonstration on 2nd
December 2008.

As I am looking out from the platform to my right hand
side, there by the pillar is a lady to whom I wish to speak.
The lady has greyish hair and wearing glasses, I am being
told that she has a very nice personality but not too sure
about the things that will be happening here this evening,
however she is willing to listen. I am being told that this
lady does not suffer fools very easily, so I am therefore
going to have to convince her that what is happening is
at least possible. In her working life the lady would have
been very well respected in her capabilities and would
have worked in some ways, speaking and teaching to the
public. I feel she has quite a lot of strings to her bow.
There is a new venture she is undertaking at this point
and it is important for her to know that she is on the
right track. She is confident in what she is doing but just
needs a bit of reassurance as the work involved will very

much help others, this is something she has wanted to do for several years but could never find the time. I feel the initial "J" would be important to her as I am seeing that being written above her head.

However I am now aware that I have a gentleman coming forward who wishes to speak with her. I feel the gentleman would be her father, he too is a man of good stature and stands tall, he is a man of good character and is very close with you, I feel he tells me that he was rather stern whilst here on the earth plane, but only ever wanted the best for you, he says he is very proud of your achievements. I also hear the name of William being called in at this time, but that would link to your father. I am also aware of a lady coming forward now who tells me she is your mother, they both stand close together and I feel very much a partnership, where one was just as important as the other, mother was a very particular lady about her appearance whilst on the earth plane and she is smiling and telling me that was important to her to be the best you could be. I am now hearing brother being called in, but I feel she means that you have a brother here on the earth plane to whom she wishes to be remembered.

Just as I am beginning to draw away from you, I feel that there is another gentleman coming forward who would have been very close to you (I feel that may have been a partner) he tells me that he passed very quickly and points to the chest area, (heart attack perhaps), I feel he is very emotional at this time and finding it rather difficult to relay the message he wants to get over, however, he says to tell you that he is closer than you think and he will communicate at another time. Take his love and know that he receives your thoughts and thanks you for them.

Second Sitting: – 10.00.a.m. Saturday 16th August 2008. to receive communication from Source Energy. (Sitting taking place at home) for demonstration on 2nd December 2008.

Right hand side, gentleman sitting in the middle of the back row, he is wearing a shirt and jacket, should also be wearing his glasses but really does not like them, he is quite a tall gentleman with a good sense of humour, who will try to make fun of me, but he really is a very serious person and hides a lot behind the humour.

I feel very strongly that there is a lady coming forward to speak with him, I feel very much a partnership, the lady tells me she was very ill before her passing and it is important that he knows she does not have that condition now and is happy to be where she is as she has the freedom to move around as she was very restricted whilst here on the earth plane. I feel this lady to be a very gentle soul and put up with your nonsense as you very much made her laugh. I am hearing her say 2 daughters and I feel she wants to be remember there. She is a very emotional lady and trying not to be too upset whilst giving me this information. She says she has waited a long time to be able to speak with you, and tells me you will have to "get your head around this idea" but to be happy in the knowledge that she is with you, and yes you can have another life, it will not change what we had, you must make the best of what you have now and keep me as a memory, you are too good to be by yourself. Just as I begin to leave you I am hearing the name Elizabeth being called in as a memory for you. Also I must tell you to take better care of your health as you are no good at doing what the Doctor ordered, you must do as you are told and things will be a lot better for you.

Now I am being told that it was a good job you put the handkerchief in your pocket before you came. Keep the memory of those you love in your head and in your heart.

Third Sitting: – 12.34.p.m. Saturday 16th August 2008. to receive communication from Source Energy. (Sitting taking place at home) for demonstration on 2nd December 2008.

Straight ahead of me at the back of the Church there is a gentleman standing, he is wearing a dark coloured suit the gentleman looks like Archie Lawrie (similar appearance) he is looking at his watch as though he expects someone to arrive late, he looks as though he is officiating, or waiting for someone to enter the room.

However I have a lady coming forward for him who tells me she is his mother, I feel a very strong bond between the both of them, she is very anxious to speak with him, to tell him she is really proud of him and the work he is doing. I also want to give the gentleman the name of Mary who would also link to him from the source energy. I feel the lady's personality to be rather quiet, but a very knowledgeable person, skilled in an academic way, has a very inquisitive mind and always seeking for answers. She says she works with you quite a lot and tries to inspire you in your work. You have been rather downhearted recently and are in need of a bit of upliftment, you let other people bring your spirit down and you must learn to be your own person. I am being told the month of November will see many changes for you and you will be able to move forward and enjoy your life more. I also have a younger lady coming forward now who is very close to you (partner) as I feel a lot of emotion as she comes forward, I feel there was a lot of difficulty with her breathing before she passed, she tells

113

me there were lots of things she wanted to say but was not able to do so because of the difficulty with her breathing. She does not have that condition now and is able to tell you she is around you a lot, but you must "cheer up" as she is not happy with you at the moment, you need to get yourself back on track. I think this lady was very supportive of you whilst she was here on the earth plane, she says you need to sit down and put your thoughts to paper and that will help you to understand the next step forward. The initial "W" has just been written above your head so that must be the name of someone close to you within the spirit realms who wishes to be remembered. I also hear someone call in "love to the 2 boys". (grandchildren). The lady says she likes the new tie you bought recently, although you have not got around to wearing it. Just know that they are all around you and only a thought away.

Fourth Sitting: – 13.08.p.m. Saturday 16th August 2008. to receive communication from Source Energy. (Sitting taking place at home) for demonstration on 2nd December 2008.

Left hand side (back row) lady white hair, wearing glasses, wearing necklace or pendant, very smart reserved lady has a very nice smile, rather shy does not really like being the centre of attention wants to hear what has to be said but wishes it was in private.

I have a gentleman coming forward for you who tells me that this is his chance to let you know that he is around you as you have been sending out many thoughts to him. I feel the gentleman to be very close (partner) and he is a bit worried about you at this time, as your health has not been good and you are somewhat tired, he says to tell you that really is what is wrong, you just need to take things easy and give yourself a "wee rest" do not let others pull you down as they are stronger and can cope by themselves. He says happy birthday for the July month and that he watched over the proceedings, there is another celebration coming up towards the end of the year around Christmas time but not Christmas itself – a family gathering. He is talking of success for a younger member of the family, I feel a young man (grandson) and I can see academic achievements for the young man, he has had a struggle but all has paid off in the end, well done. There is also a move in the family for someone they are going overseas to live, you must not be too disappointed as that is a good move and you will see them again. He says you have been holding on to the purse strings recently, trying to gather some money together for a break, he says that will happen and you will have a great time.

I am being told that I have your father coming forward now who has a very different personality from the last gentleman. I feel he was a very hard working man, things were very scarce in his day, trying to keep the family on not too much income, it was hard but worth every minute, he says his kids were his pride and joy and would have done anything for you all. I feel he talks of a brother in the spirit world with him who also wishes to be remembered to you, a lot of happy memories. There are also 2 dogs that were in the family when you were a youngster. I feel he is trying to show me your home, as I am in a room with quite a few pictures on the wall, but I feel that to be a sitting room, as he says he draws close to you in that room whilst you sit and ponder your thoughts.

You also have a photograph album that you look at now and then, he also has memories of someone playing the piano, and I feel you must have a photograph of that, a lot of happy thoughts within that room. Just as I begin to leave you, I hear a lady say, I am her mother and I want to speak with her for a moment, I feel the lady is rather frail as she comes forward and that would be her last memory before passing, she just wants you to know that she is close and thanks you for all you did for her whilst she was here. Take all her love and know that they are all around you supporting you and holding your thoughts together.

Fifth Sitting:- 11.05.p.m Thursday 21st August 2008 to receive communication from Source Energy. (Sitting taking place at home) for demonstration on 2nd December 2008.

Left side near the front 2nd row there is a lady with whom I wish to speak she has dark hair and the colour red would be quite strong around her, I feel I am being told that the colour red is for strength for her as she has been through a rough time over the past few months, she is here with a friend, but her friend has only come to support her. She is very emotional at this time and also a very shy lady but she will be glad to speak with me.

I am her father and we were very close whilst I was here on the earth plane and was rather ill before my passing and she helped me greatly, now I have come to support her and to tell her all will be well, it will take approximately 2 months to see a difference in the health situation around her. I also want to speak about her mother who is in the spirit world with myself, I am aware that your father is trying to bring your mother forward now as I feel the lady would have been very frail before her passing and she talks of this only to confirm that it is her, and that she is well, and with your father. Your father is now bringing a gentleman forward who tells me he passed very quickly (heart attack) and is very close with you (partner) he tells me that it would be too emotional for yourself to deal with him contacting you for too long as the memories you have are still very fresh with you and he does not want to bring anything forward at a public demonstration but assures you he is close with you and yes he does hear your thoughts and is trying to help you. You must keep your chin up and take each day as it comes. He says love to the boys they are a great support. He shows me the initial "J" being put above your head and he wants to be remembered there with fond memories. He says at this time hope is your greatest friend and he will return to speak to you when the time is right.

Happy birthday.

Sixth Sitting:- 11.30.p.m Thursday 21st August 2008 to receive communication from Source Energy. (Sitting taking place at home) for demonstration on 2nd December 2008.

Right hand side towards the back on the right side of the row 2 or 3 chairs in I want to speak with the lady wearing glasses and a watch which belonged to her mother the initial "A" would be important to her. I am her father.

I have a rather stern looking gentleman coming forward for you and he says do not be deceived by my appearance I am just a big softy at heart.

He tells me that you need his strength at this time to go forward as there are many things going on in your life at this time and you need some answers as you do not know which way to turn, he says all will be dealt with within the next 2-3weeks and things will be much improved for you. He is bringing an aunt in for you with a lot of happy memories with this lady, he tells me she draws close to you to give you support. I am hearing the name of William being called in now and I feel that is also a family connection. Your father is bringing forward a child in the spirit world who wishes to link with you very closely. As he begins to leave you now I am hearing the name of Tom being called in, also there would have been someone in a wheelchair for a time before their passing and that would in some way link to the name of Tom. I am also hearing someone say mother-in-law and I feel she was in hospital before her passing as I feel that to be a last memory with her and she wants you to know that she is o.k. now and a big thank you for your support, as she says she was not very good at expressing her feelings whilst she was here on the earth plane.

There are many souls who surround you and are sending healing thoughts at this time.

Seventh Sitting:- 11.55.p.m Thursday 21st August 2008 to receive communication from Source Energy. (Sitting taking place at home) for demonstration on 2nd December 2008.

Right hand side front row two ladies sitting together (friends) I want to speak with the more rounded lady on my right hand side. The lady has a great sense of humour and will not be offended when you say that. I have to say that you like sweeties (in your handbag) and you usually try and sneak one or two during the demonstration.

I have two gentlemen coming forward for you and I am finding it quite difficult to separate them at the moment as both of them think that they have the right to speak first, however I am hearing them say that you are no stranger to this sort of communication and you would understand there sense of humour. I feel I have a father and a partner both coming forward but I think your father is the one speaking first as he was a very strong character and really just wants to assure you that he is still around you and watches over you. He says he is bringing forward with him your friend's partner as he has not been through before and needs a wee bit of help with his communication, I feel this gentleman to be of a much gentler nature and quite reserved (would not wear his heart of his sleeve) so to speak but just wants you to know that he is o.k. and says thank you for all the lovely flowers, as I think he also means that he liked to be in his garden. He says he was very frail before his passing and lost a lot of weight as he had difficulty eating and swallowing. He say you talk to his picture just before you go to sleep and he wants you to know that he says the same things back (but he would not tell me what that is) none of my business. He is taking of a wedding ring and handing it to you and says you will understand the significance, he says it should be worn.

Take care of the dog.

Eighth Sitting:- 11.35.pm Thursday 23rd October 2008 to receive communication from Source Energy. (Sitting taking place at home) for demonstration on 2nd December 2008.

Far left back row (near in the corner) lady who has whitish hair, but something colourful around her shoulders, has a cardigan on, she is feeling the cold these days, has her arms folded.

I am hearing mother being called in now, and I feel I have a lady with me who is rather anxious to speak with you; she wants to tell you that you must follow the Dr.'s instructions at this time. You have not been doing what you have been told to do and therefore have had to suffer the consequences, but if you do as you are told everything will work out. I also feel I have father coming forward now and he is a very gentle soul but also a no nonsense man, but gives you all the support you need at this time, you must think of yourself just now and he wants to help you to do that. You are getting yourself in a "pickle" because you just do not like thinking of yourself and that is alien to you.

He is giving me the initial "J" for you as a memory just to clarify who is around you at this time, he says you are a wonderful human being but are not always recognised as this. I am hearing daughter being called in for you and I feel I have a young person, who tells me she died just after touching the earth plane but has grown up in the Spirit World, I also feel an anniversary in the month of November (she says just past). She is laughing and talking about "baking Christmas Cake" and I feel she watches over you a lot and laughs at some of the things you do.

I am hearing someone talk about a grandson to tell you he is very fond of you and "loves you to bits". (But I think he is here on the earth plane)

However I am being told that they have all come because of the urgency to tell you to "do what you are told" for once. I am hearing the name of Peter being called in but also seeing the initial "P" being written up for you.

Take their love and know that they surround you to guide and help you.

Communications completed

TESTIMONIALS FOR DECEMBER EXPERIMENT

Comments by A.A. Lawrie on SCORING:-

Average Score for Descriptions = 86%
Average score for Acceptance of Messages = 78%

1. Descriptions of the Sitters.

Of the 8 descriptions given (months in advance) by the medium regarding the seating positions that the audience members would take up, as well as the physical descriptions of the sitters, 7 such declarations scored 100%. The remaining two scored 50% and 87.5%.

No matter how we look at such a score, it is a truly astonishing result. In fact it is so high that it looks fictitious although we know that it is truly genuine.

The fact that any medium, anywhere, can produce such a score <u>months in advance</u> with a public audience that is completely unknown to her, really means that we have to look extremely seriously as to the meaning of what we usually call, "free will".

The fact that this psychic medium has produced such a result TWICE OVER in the same year only adds to the wonder of the situation.

2. Messages for the Sitters.

While 78% is not as good as 86% correctness, it is still a hugely impressive score.

As a researcher, I would have been happy with half of such a score!

3. An Unusual and Unexpected Situation.

The scoring was complicated by the fact that "Sitter 7" turned out to be two good friends and not a single sitter at all! This was only discovered after the test was carried out and as the strangeness of the scoring for that sheet was being analysed.

It was almost as if the spirit world threw in that case to let us see that a 'pair' of people could come through the system as if they were one single human entity.

This psychic medium should be exceedingly pleased that her dedicated work has produced such excellent and interesting results for psychical research.

Archibald A. Lawrie
Professional Psychical Researcher
The President, The Edinburgh Society for Psychical Research
Vice-President, The Scottish Society for Psychical Research

SECTION 8

Answers to twenty fun questions.

Answers to psychic/mediumistic development quiz.

ANSWERS TO TWENTY FUN QUESTIONS

Are you a sensitive?

Yes, of course you are we are all sensitive; as we are born with the ability and can develop it further if we choose. It is quite simple really, if you take the time to get to know yourself and listen to yourself, whereby you become in tune with what is in, and around you, then you will start to feel more for others, as you raise your emotional levels to connect to the universe, making you a more contented, relaxed, happy, healthy, wealthy, reachable person. Does that sound like you? –Soon will be if you allow yourself the time to let it happen.

Do you know who you really are?

You are source energy encased within a physical body for the period of time you wish to spend upon this earth plane. I can hear a lot of bells ringing and you not being too sure what are meant by source energies. That is a subject that needs to be covered in depth and I would suggest to you, if you wish to find out more, then you can look through my website, which will give you at least some answers, then perhaps you may wish to dig a little bit deeper, whereby you can contact me personally with your questions. Happy digging.

Do you know what intuition is?

That's a simple one, it is of course your own gut feelings about things, a hunch, an insight or just a knowing when situations around you seem to be good, bad or indifferent, when all your warning bells are ringing for no apparent reasons, other than your intuition trying to inform you to pay attention to your inner thoughts and act upon them.

Do you meditate?

The answer, of course should be YES. Hopefully you are now practising daily meditation – section 1 page 11.

Do you use visualisation exercises at any time?

These exercises will help you to still the mind and allow you to practise focusing your thoughts on one thing at a time, therefore allowing yourself the discipline needed to become more attuned to your own source energy. If you are a beginner, I would ask you to have the patience to sit and the dedication to find what works best for you, in as much as, what visualisation method you would use. I think a good simple one, is just to focus on your breathing thereby becoming more relaxed and able to release all your material thoughts for that short period of time. The good thing about that is, you do not need to spend lots of money on visualisation tapes, c.d.'s, whatever.

Are you aware of universal energies?

What is meant by that is – Do you believe that we survive the death of the physical body. If the answer is yes then you might well believe it is possible to communicate with the discarnate energy.

Do you believe in a discarnate supreme being?

The question is, do you believe in a God, or whatever name you call your God, for many people that is their understanding of the after-life and see God as a person with a physical body. Which of course, I have my own thoughts on, and they are certainly not that God is a person.

Can you contact your inner-self?

Simply, yes with a little dedication, patience, and allowing yourself time for that to happen, just by following the simple exercises of meditation, visualisation, and relaxation. In other words chill-out.

Are you telepathic?

Telepathy is of the conscious mind and does not require speech. It is only when we wish to pass information between each other that we use the voice. Here is another thought for you. I believe, when the universe began and early man first inhabited the earth plane, we did not speak.

We communicated through thoughts – scary. We only found it necessary to speak as we evolved and therefore lost the art of telepathy. I have no way of proving this, it is only my hypothesis.

If you have pets, you will relate to this as they communicate easily with you in order to have their needs met.

Do you have an aura?

Yes, most definitely, the aura is the life-force of the physical body, it can be seen by some people, and it can also be picked-up on a very special camera, which will show the auric field in colour. This is the energy field we use as psychics and channels to read what is going on in your life, as we read the colours that surround you, an electro magnetic force field, so I am told, but it is really quite simple, as that is your life force and when you die it is part of you that goes forward to join the universal consciousness and leaves behind the physical body which we no longer have any use for.

Are you a good judge of character?

The answer would be self-explanatory, either you are or you are not. If yes then that is a bonus, as you have your own built-in warning system. If no then you need to practise working more on your intuition, sorry, but make that a journey of joy.

Do you believe the consciousness lives on after the death of the physical body?

Well, of course, you have freedom of choice, as you either believe that consciousness survives after death of the physical body or you do not. However, that is where your search for truths may begin, happy searching. For me it would most definitely be a YES as that is what my work is all about, to try to prove survival of the consciousness after we die. I am sure you will come to some sort of conclusion in your own time. But if I can help with any development issues then please contact me for a reading.

Is it possible to foresee the future?

Under certain circumstances, I know, for me it is possible to clarify that, please see my section on Paranormal Research. This is a rather in-depth subject and only for those who have the foresight to believe that it could be attainable and are willing to search for answers. Please let me know if you have any success. This section is really for the serious paranormal researcher.

Do you know what precognition is?

An extra-sensory ability to foresee a future event, for example clairvoyance the seeing within one's mind what may happen. In some cases this will happen during the dream-state or some other altered state of consciousness.

Do you think you have lived a previous life?

Really what is being asked is do you believe in reincarnation? I personally have my own points of view on that one, as I have no previous knowledge of any past lives, so far, and never really felt the need to go backwards in my life, as I am a very forward thinking person, always seeking to what might be in the future. But that does not mean to say that would be your experiences.

Have you ever been under hypnosis?

I mean by that have you ever consulted a Hypnotherapist by appointment. I rather think the general opinion would be no. But I must tell you that you have in all probability been in a hypnotic state at some point in your life, as hypnosis only means an altered state of consciousness which can be achieved by different methods i.e. intentionally by alcohol, drugs, anaesthetic, so on, and of course by suggestion from a Hypnotherapist when you seek a session. Some people think the therapist is in control of your mind, but that could not be further from the truth as only you can control your mind. Under hypnosis you are totally aware of everything being said, your free will cannot be taken from you therefore you will not do anything that goes against your nature.

Do you believe it is possible to cure yourself of certain illnesses?

Yes, I think in some circumstances the power of positive thinking can bring about a physical change.

Do you believe that the mind is more powerful than the physical body?

Bearing in mind all that we have said about the consciousness, I believe for me there is only one answer, YES for we hold the greatest power there is as human beings, within our mind. I believe as such we have only scratched the surface in connection with what the mind is possible of achieving. So go play your mind games and see what you can achieve.

Do you believe that there is a parallel universe?

By far the most complex question to answer. I think it's easy to talk about our life experience. I myself am in no doubt that our thoughts are in more than one universe and we can communicate with the consciousness of the other on many different levels. It is only when we experience these things for ourselves that we begin to understand we are more than mere mortals. We hold the greatest power within, our consciousness, for that is the part that can communicate on many levels. We humans find it very hard to believe the things we do not understand as we have a great need to label everything. However, I am striving to prove that the unbelievable can become believable.

It is sometimes difficult and always intriguing to try to understand what really should be second nature to us all.

Are you really sure you want to further develop your psychic awareness?

Hopefully you have all said yes as the more this earth plane becomes attuned to The Source, then the easier it will become for us all to live together in peace and harmony to enhance our lives.

15 -20 Excellent:
10 -15 Very Good:
5 – 10 Good:
0 – 5 You can still work with that, you are on the right pathway.

ANSWERS TO PSYCHIC/MEDIUMISTIC DEVELOPMENT QUIZ.

Should psychic/mediumistic development should be open to anyone?

False:
You must first establish that the person wishing to develop is in the correct mental state. I.e. not on any type of medication for mental illnesses. Is of sound mind and as far as you are aware good character.

Do you have to be psychic to become a medium?

True:
All mediums are psychic but not all psychics are mediums.

Would you attempt to first make your mind clear when sitting for development?

True:
All development becomes easier when you are in a state of meditation, allowing your mind to be still.

Can a medium follow any religion they choose?

True:
Mediumship embraces all religions, caste, colour and creed and does not discriminate.

Should you encourage a developing medium to work with their eyes closed?

False:
This in the long-term would only hinder the developing medium as they would have to re-train themselves when doing public demonstrations of mediumship, as your eyes will help you place the person with whom you want to speak. Unless, of course the developing medium has impaired sight to begin with and their training would have to be done differently.

Can you sit in different development circles as often as you please?

True:
It is my opinion that you can sit whenever and wherever you choose, as your development is your responsibility and you have freedom of choice as to what suits you best. I am sure you have all heard the saying "One man's meat is another man's poison". Although not all tutors would agree with me, it is important that you find the correct tutor for you.

Would you ever apologise for your mediumship?

False:
By the very nature of how communication takes place, it would be impossible to have everything correct, as we are dealing with a very fine tuned organ, our mind.

Would you always give evidence of communicator?

True:
That is a medium's job, to prove survival after the death of the physical body. You must strive to make the

communication as clear and accurate as possible, but at the same time remembering that you can only ever be a channel for the communication and try to keep your thoughts out of the way.

Whilst sitting in development circles how clear are you of what type of mediumship you wish to have?

False:
You do not know when you first sit for development what may come forward for you, so you must always have an open-mind and be willing to try everything you receive until you find a happy medium, so to speak.

Do you have to have spiritual knowledge to develop physical phenomena?

False:
There are people who can produce physical phenomena without any knowledge of spiritual matters and in many cases have been the best mediums we have and therefore able to produce wonderful evidence of survival of the human spirit.

When in trance the mind of the medium is highly active?

True:
All communications come through the mind of the medium, as in the case of mental mediumship and physical mediumship, the mind is the bridge for the communications to take place.

Do you think you should ever question what your tutor tells you.

True:

Only if your tutor is Beatrice McCaig. Of course it is FALSE you must always make sure you have an understanding of what is being taught, so therefore you must not be embarrassed to ask questions, after all we are all learning new things every day, even tutors do not have all the answers.

TESTIMONIALS

Beatrice is a gifted and caring medium.

She has given hope inspiration and encouragement to many, through bleak times. And enabled them to have a thankful rather than despairing heart.

Kay Ogilvie,
President, Edinburgh Association of Spiritualists.

***

A genuine, caring, sincere and honest psychic medium.

Beatrice is a master of her craft. a straight talking lady with her feet firmly on the ground, who provides accurate information and evidence from her spirit communicators. There is only one word I can use to describe my reading with this lady WOW.

Beatrice thank you so much.

Kind regards and much love.

Donna Crozier,
Edinburgh.

***

I can say with full confidence that I have never met a more sincere medium than Beatrice McCaig; Beatrice is truly dedicated, not only to her field of work, but to the honest progression of it.

I met Beatrice 5 years ago now after a mediumistic demonstration where she gave me amazing communication from my late great grandmother. Later I was lucky enough to spend 9 months learning in one of her development circles here in Spain. She taught me how to find myself, at the deepest and most truthful level, while keeping a light and fun atmosphere. There was never any place in her circle for being, in her own words, "wired to the moon", we were taught to stay grounded while lovingly encouraged to progress, each at our own pace.

Beatrice excels at keeping the highest level of professionalism with her work. In a field where there are no real foundational rules of practice, she sets an exemplary standard.

I want to take this opportunity Beatrice to say Thank You, I would never have achieved the success I have in my inner and outer worlds without your guidance and friendship.......

Leona Jancie Graham,
Spain.

***

I have known Beatrice for twenty years.

We first met in a Development Circle, we joined with others to develop our mediumship. It was very evident to me that even then she had a natural gift in helping others to cope with various traumas in their lives by bringing messages forward from the Spirit World to help and comfort them, and to prove without doubt that there is life after physical death.

Her mediumship has gone from strength to strength over the years, she is an honest, forthright and genuine lady whom I would have no hesitation in recommending when in need of spiritual help.

Irene Coull,
Port Seton, Scotland.

***

I have known Beatrice for many years.

Where I have been fortunate to witness her work, within the church and on a private level. Beatrice is a honest and humble person who tends to minimise her gift. Beatrice or should I say B (the name I use for her) has always been passionate about her work and is always willing to take it to another level in seeking the answer we all desire.

For many years she has dedicated her own personal time in developing herself into an excellent medium and healer she is today, and has also helped other people to explore their own capabilities to develop their gift. She is an excellent teacher who is always more than willing to go the extra mile for someone who generally needs her help and guidance. What must be remembered is that B has also managed to successfully be wife and mother whilst committing her life to the spirit world in order for voices to be heard from the universal life force we all known is there.

Namaste to all who read this and good luck B with your new journey in providing the answers.

Angela Grady, Halifax.

***

Four years ago I had the pleasure of meeting Beatrice.

I had a reading from her which was 3 years after I had lost my husband of 33 years in a car accident.

I was still very emotional but was trying to move on with my life. She indicated through my late husband that I was to move on and gave me his blessing. This was a tremendous relief to me, that my husband approved of what I was about to embark on.

She also referred to a pair of earnings in a box which I had not worn. I did not know of any but was given a present that afternoon of earrings in a box which had been bought that morning about the time of my reading !!

Beatrice also mentioned quite a few personal things that were not possible for her to have known which was very surprising. She is a very genuine lady and certainly helped me through a troubling time.

Joan,
Scotland

***

I first met Beatrice about fifteen years ago.

She was the founder of my local Spiritualist Church and she was the medium that night. Later on in my development, I was privileged to have her as my Tutor. I was inspired by her teaching and the way in which she encouraged her students with both her knowledge and frankness and no nonsense attitude to all things spiritual. Always endeavouring to enable her students to have a richer experience to their spiritual enfoldment.

Yvonne Craig,
Port Seton, Scotland.

***

Hi Beatrice,

Just like to say thank you for all the help and inspiration you have given me over the years. I really appreciate your directness in the readings you have given me, they seem to always clarify life and the way forward as well as giving me an "understanding" of how it all works!!..

WB
Spain.

***

Beatrice is the most straight talking down to earth person/medium I know. She tells it as it is and could never be accused of being wired to the moon. There was a time where I was getting a lot of messages from the platform telling me that they (the person giving said message) could see a break-up and that I was going to be splitting up with my husband. Now being the type of person I am I did not take any of this to heart which is lucky. The only medium who said I was family orientated and I would do anything to protect my family was Beatrice. 15 years on I am still with my husband and the kids are going from strength to strength.

I have also attended classes that Beatrice has run which have been both fun and educational. She encourages you to progress at your own pace and helps you to feel an important part of the group irrespective of your ability. She is a lovely lady and it is my pleasure to know her.

Corrie McGill,
Edinburgh.